DATE DUE

NO 3 '95			
MY 3 0 '96			
FE 26 '98			
AP 17 0			
NO 1			

New Chicana/Chicano Writing

N E W
CHICANA/
CHICANO
W R I T I N G

3

Charles M. Tatum, Editor

THE UNIVERSITY OF ARIZONA PRESS

Tucson & London

CHARLES M. TATUM is professor of Spanish and head of the Department of Spanish and Portuguese at the University of Arizona, where he also teaches Chicano and Latin American literature. He has published extensively in the areas of Chicano literature, Latin American literature, and Latin American popular culture. He is author of *Chicano Literature* (1982), translated and published in Spanish in 1986. Tatum was also for several years editor of publications of the *Latin American Literary Review*. He is coeditor of the journal, *Studies in Latin American Popular Culture*.

Partial funding for this book was provided by the Arizona Commission on the Arts through appropriations from the Arizona State Legislature and grants from the National Endowment for the Arts.

The University of Arizona Press
Copyright © 1993
Arizona Board of Regents
All Rights Reserved

⊗ This book is printed on acid-free, archival-quality paper.
Manufactured in the United States of America.

98 97 96 95 94 93   6 5 4 3 2 1

New Chicana/Chicano writing
ISSN 1058-2770

Contents

Introduction

The third volume of "New Chicana/Chicano Writing," like its preceding two companion volumes, offers a variety of previously unpublished creative literary works by both relatively well-known writers as well as by those who will not be as familiar to most readers. Several contributors to this present volume appeared previously in volumes I and II; they include Joel Huerta, Pat Mora, Raúl Niño, Rita Magdaleno, Orlando Ramírez, and Odilia Galván Rodríguez. The remaining contributors—Rolando Hinojosa, Dan Cooper Alarcón, Patricia Blanco, Carlos Cumpián, Roberta Fernández, Stephen D. Gutiérrez, Ana Perches, Mary Helen Ponce, and Diego Vásquez, Jr.— are new to the series. All of the contributors' prose narrative works, poetry, and personal essays were selected after careful editorial consideration from more than one hundred manuscripts submitted.

We have tried to remain faithful to the spirit and criteria that have guided the series from the beginning: to present high quality literary works representative of the great breadth and wide variety of creative literature by Chicana and Chicano writers. Readers looking for specific themes, language use, rhetoric, and tone based on preconceived—and outmoded—notions of what they think should constitute Chicano literature, will probably be disappointed. Chicana and Chicano writing today defies rigid categories and cannot be contained within prescribed boundaries. Just as the multiple experiences, lifestyles, and cultural and linguistic complexities of people of Mexican descent across the Southwest and across the country do not lend themselves to simplistic descriptive formulas, our literature is correspondingly diverse. In making often difficult decisions on what to include and what to exclude from this third volume, we have been guided mainly by aesthetic considerations and not by what we thought readers and critics might prefer. The following selections do not conform to a strict litmus test of acceptable topics and content. To allow ourselves to be guided by such narrow considerations would ultimately be a great disservice to today's literature by Chicana and Chicano writers.

The prose narrative works contained in this volume amply reflect a wide range of modes and themes. Joel Huerta and Stephen D. Gutiérrez's contributions, both excerpts from novels in progress, use satire to explore serious themes. Huerta's work is linear and traditional in terms of point of view while Gutiérrez's is wildly experimental in its narrative structure. Huerta examines two worlds, one Anglo, one Chicano, that inhabit the same geographical space yet barely touch each other in a more profound cultural way. In his satirical narrative "Unfurled," he pokes fun at an ambitious young Anglo woman who idealizes an attractive Chicano male, fitting him into her romanticized notion of Hispanic culture. At the same time, Huerta is gently critical of an older Mexican-American generation that clings tenaciously to its material possessions as symbols of social status. Gutiérrez uses his fictional character, Walter C. Ramírez, an aspiring creative writing professor, as a vehicle to expose lingering racism, sexism, and antisemitism within the university. Gutiérrez uses humor to express seething rage and alienation. Ramírez vents his angst through a series of fictional letters to a newspaper editor. Rolando Hinojosa revisits the theme of war in his writing, first seen in his long narrative poem *Korean Love Songs* (1978). "A Spring Break," excerpted from a novel in progress, is a first-person account of the day-to-day drudgery of fighting a war stripped of its glorious reconstructions and nostalgic memories. Roberta Fernández's "Double Talk" traverses two geographic regions, the first a Third World underdeveloped Central American country, the second a highly developed First World region of the American Southwest. Commonalities rather than differences, however, bring these two seemingly disparate areas together as she traces a refugee's flight from political repression and his trek across Mexico to the U.S.-Mexico border. Using an interesting alternation between Spanish and English to capture the linguistic and cultural ambience of each region, Fernández weaves a tale about trust, misperceptions, and the complexity of life along the border made more tenuous by the escalation in drug smuggling. Dan Cooper Alarcón's "Shortchanged" is a finely rendered short story that explores a teenager's emotional maturation as he struggles to come to grips with the electrocution of his friend, a young deaf mute half his age, while at the same time working through a difficult relationship with both his parents. Cooper Alarcón subtly develops his character's transition from adolescent self-centeredness to his increasing awareness of others. As other Chicana writers have only recently begun to do, Ana Perches boldly explores the different dimensions of male, and particularly, female sexuality in her short narrative work, "Venus Envy." Using a fragmented conversation between a woman and two men, Perches brings to the surface reflections on sexuality rarely dealt with so explicitly by other Chicana or Chicano writers. Mary Helen Ponce's personal essay "On Writing" is a richly detailed and sensitive plumbing of her reasons for writing and how they relate to the experiences of growing up Chicana, commitment to a social agenda, and her dedication to feminism. Her reflections explore the natural role that writing plays in her textured life.

The poetry selections in this volume are every bit as varied in theme and language as the prose narrative works. Featured are three Tucson poets, Patricia Blanco and Rita Magdaleno, who reside in this culturally diverse Southwestern city, and Orlando Ramírez, who was born here. Blanco's highly introspective poetry reminds us of some of César Vallejo's "Poemas humanos" in their striking incorporation of everyday things that surround and remind the poet of painful absences, the finiteness of joy and love, and the futility of violence in the

name of some political ideology. Her imagery is sharply evoca-
tive. Magdaleno's autobiographical poems draw on memories
of family, places and experiences from childhood, including the burial of an infant sister, her war-bride mother, the
warmth of a young girl's friends, and the parallels between
political boundaries and those separating daughter from
mother. While a few of Ramírez's poems are, like those of
Blanco and Magdaleno, reflective and questioning in a personal way, most of the ones selected for this volume have a
wider focus in the sense that they address broad themes, such
as the difficulty of cultural identity in an increasingly com-
modified, postmodern American society. His view of the direction our culture seems to be taking is one of foreboding.
Some of the poetry by Carlos Cumpián, Diego Vásquez, Jr.,
Odilia Galván Rodríguez, and Raúl Niño also touches on
broad cultural themes, but these poets demonstrate great sensitivity in exploring intimate, personal themes as well. Verbal
skill and sensitivity to nuance characterize all of the poets included in the anthology.

As in the first and second anthologies in the series, readers
will find in the following pages humor and pathos, joy and
sadness, acceptance and protest, introspection, and focus on
social themes. We hope there is something for every reader.

JOEL HUERTA

Unfurled

Houston, Texas 1963

The day after Charlamaigne Overcash had graduated from the
Teacher's College of Houston, she and her girlfriends were on
an airplane bound for Acapulco, Mexico. Dancing on a bal-
cony planted on the Costera, she had declared to her Acapul-
can beau, Julio César Rust: "Julio, I may never ever return to
Texas."

The next morning Charlamaigne was on the airplane playing canasta with the sunburnt teachers. "Girls, let's do this
again!" "Yi dawgee, we will!"

Charlamaigne Overcash was at work the next day. As part
of her General Business 312 requirement, she had interned in
the general ledger department of one of the glassy and mod-
ern Bank of Texas branches. Everyone had liked her plenty. At
her going away party at the Steak and Ale, Ray Nettles of personnel surprisingly asked, "Would you like to join the B.O.T.
team, permanently?" The maître d' ignited the coed's Bananas
Foster. "Count me in," she said, and she blew the sweet flame
out.

"Here, here!"

She liked her bank job okay. The pay was a bit above average.
She had a little work station where she could put up photos, a
calendar, dried flowers, postcards. Her co-workers were really
nice, too. They'd get together and play records and Yahtzee
and maybe go out for a drink at the Shamrock Hotel, the one
the real "Giant" built. At the Shamrock they'd mingle with

the executive types, the astronauts, they'd joke and cut rug.

From her desk on the bank mezzanine, she had been afforded a good view of the teller booth transactions. She considered herself a professional "peoplewatcher." It helped her pass the time. She liked to imagine from where they came and the kinds of houses they kept.

She had dreamt him. Breakers. Striped swim trunks. The #9 in his hand. She'd seen Orlando Palacios come and go from the bank on Friday afternoons—always after 1:00, never later than 3:00. He was well-tanned and had big green eyes, and he wore understated clothes—the truly wealthy always wore understated clothes.

He seemed polite, gentle, always talking longer than necessary. And because he was clean and pretty, because he had stature, those waiting in line behind him rarely seemed to mind. She dreamt about him even in the hubbub of the working day. She thought she had seen him once in one of those little English sports cars. At the first break in the median on Westheimer Road, she had U-turned her Belvedere, squealing tire in pursuit, but the little green car had vanished into a tunnel of oaks.

It was part of the job. It was part of Boom Town. I mean, Bank of Texas employees snooped into people's coffers all the time, but that day when Charlamaigne walked down the airy metal and gold-flecked stone staircase to check the gentleman's name and account number, so that she might then peek into that T.D. & H's file, it was the handcuff of fate she felt lock onto her wrist, not guilt. No, it wasn't guilt. How could it be guilt? She was *authorized.*

Yet somewhere along her descent from the mezzanine to the buzzing lobby, she felt her bank-day reality bleach out. She gripped the banister. She had to pause for twenty or thirty seconds. She felt like a kite tangled in a palm tree where the gulf wind is gusting. The sensation was, of course, the forebearer of love, the *right* kind of lust; it was the bitter berry taste found on the tongue of the aiming hunter.

Some tender-voiced and strong-armed being helped her down the stairs and across the bank to her destination. "Come now, Charlamaigne. You so desire this gentleman, so git on with it. Take him. Fear not the man. Git on down there."

She had not seen the Samaritan's face. She had assumed it had been Montclair, the whistling, Old Spice-smelling security chief, but when she asked Montclair the next day, Montclair said "Nope. It waddunt me." And it wasn't Eddie or Rob or Big Sue. No breathin' human could remember assisting her. It remains a mystery.

Charlamaigne found herself tapping on the teller's shoulder. "What was that one tall gentleman's name?" she asked.

"Oh, the one with . . ."

"Yeah, that gypsy-lookin' fella."

"Miss Overcash, are you alright?" The teller began pulling on her earring nervously.

"Yes, why yes, yes," Charlamaigne said.

"You've got red splotches all over here." The teller pointed to Charlamaigne's neck and cleavage. She pressed into Charlamaigne's splotches with her Bank of Texas pencil eraser. Charlamaigne could see no splotches. She saw sunlight on saltwater. An aluminum surf. The #9. That's all she saw.

"I'd bet my bottom dollar that's oyster rash. Let me see. Oh yeah, that's oyster rash," a customer informed.

"And that gentleman's name?" Charlamaigne managed.

"They're getting redder."

"Yup, that's oyster rash. It's gonna spread."

"I *need* that gentleman's name!"

Palacios, Orlando Jesús. 059958. Code 5. It surprised her that he was Spanish. Orlando Jesús Palacios. Spanish. Golden matador waving crimson cape on black velvet night. Orlando Palacios of the Christ Child Jesus of Nazareth, blessed be thy name on earth as it is in heaven for thine is the kingdom, and power, and glory, amen.

Floors of gold, inlaid mother of pearl and bells tolling above and strumming guitars below. She and Orlando, they would dance, snapping fingers, tap tapping 'round the lip of a fountain. Oh, Don Orlando Palacios of Jesu–kneeling before her, offering a ring on the tip of a dagger. Orlando, Picasso, stain-glassy, starry through her black, lace-covered señorita eyes.

That evening Charlamaigne Overcash ended up on the 36th floor of the brand new Regency Hotel's Club La Comete. From below, the club looked like a domed conservatory or an enormous igloo. From within, the Houston set could see their city lights, and their brighter constellations. They could see a melancholy, more transitory reflection of themselves on the mercuric glass walls of the neighboring Texaco Tower. It was a lovely, lovely place. But Charlamaigne Overcash was not at La Comete for sunsets and bird's-eye views of Houston. She was not there to gaze out at the speeding stars; she was not there to kiss an acquaintance's cheek howdy; she was there for some private business.

She had withdrawn $25 from her account at B.O.T. Three fives and ten singles kept handy for the greasing of palms at the "European-style hotel." Her rich Aunt Lue had taken her there once before. Charlamaigne also had her emergency $50 folded and stashed between a picture of her squinting family on a motorboat off Galveston and another photo of her mother Tillie. And finally, she had a dime taped to the back of her watch—emergency phone money.

Charlamaigne ordered "a Manhattan, no a Tom Collins." She gave the waiter a five and he brought back no change. She sipped her Tom Collins and lit a cigarette. She didn't really smoke so she blew out instead of sucking. She tapped off some ashes. Yes, one or two of those 500,000 lights out there in the Space City belonged to Orlando Jesús's villa, or roadster or just-lit Cuban cigar. And those traffic lights at the crossroads were his—green, gold, red . . . green, gold, red.

As the last of the day's orange faded, she came to realize that what she felt was indeed guilt. It wasn't fate. It was plain ol' guilt. And it hadn't been ignited by her looking into that man's confidentials. Everyone in banks and on streets and on steaming beds does that every day, will do that. It's a human thing. A perfectly human thing. All it takes is one real look into a person's eyes and you get *the confidentials*. Weakness, shame, strength, luck. In a book her mother Tillie had given her, Dr. Norman Vincent Peale talked about opening the treasure chest of the human soul, a.k.a *the confidentials*.

No, she didn't feel remorse about digging for gold. The $71,000 in Mr. Palacios' account could just as well have been $20,000. Get it? It was his name and identity. The person. The shoulders. The taste of it on her tongue. *Orlando Jesús Palacios*. Money was not the nugget for which she mined. End of argument.

"Another Tom Collins, please." Though she could hear her mother's voice wrangling "Oil & water, ladies & liquor—thems don't mix," though mother harangued daughter, it was time. She signaled the waiter. "Excuse me, monsieur, where's the house phone?" The waiter lifted his index finger, said something like "blek," blinked and walked away.

He brought her a heavy lavender phone on an aqua anodized aluminum platter. It was a push button phone! Charlamaigne propped the handset and held it with her shoulder and neck. "You're sitting there like nothing more than a well-dressed whore," her mother Tillie piped in—this time through the telephone.

A few tourists tried not to stare at her. They had hoped to see some A-rabs with the robes and turbans and sunglasses, but the young attractive rich woman drinking liquor alone and making phone deals would have to do.

"Honey, do you think she's an oil baroness, a real estate queen, Miss Ship Channel, Miss Houston?"

Charlamaigne liked what she heard, she liked it indeed. To hell with mother. To hell with the south. She was Diana of the goddamned hunt.

Charlamaigne knocked the ice around in her glass and took a large drink. "This one's for you mama." The beautiful woman reflected on the mirrored skyscraper next door, repeated her every move, just nanoseconds later. The two raised their tumblers high, toasted, and drank.

Dr. Tom Collins chilled her shoulders and bones, and he warmed her tongue, and the good doctor washed the grit off her heart. She had not been a drinking woman previous.

She dialed KB2–7477.

"Hello, we've got balls, how may I help you?" She hung up quickly. She checked her number again.

"Hello, we've got balls! How may I help you?"

It had to be him.

Was it really him? That conniving Dr. Collins had made a kaleidoscope of her senses.

It had to be him. He had a little accent.

"Hello? Hello? We've got balls," the man said politely. "3.99 a bucket, anytime. Ten bucks for three."

She said "guess where I'm calling from."

"Who are you?"

"Guess where I'm calling you from?"

"Who is this?"

"It's . . . It's Carmen."

"Carmen from over in the ranch?"

"No, it's pretty Carmen, Carmen from Madrid."

"Ma drid?"

"Guess where I'm calling from?"

"Your house?"

"No."

"Ma drid?"

"No."

"From Club La Comete. You know where that is." She dropped the heavy handset onto the phone's cradle. It clanked much too loudly. The harpist missed a stroke.

"It's at the Regency Hotel. Do you need golf balls?" but the line was dead.

The waiter set down a drink Charlamaigne didn't remember ordering. But what did it matter? She'd drink it.

She had to break out her emergency $50. She tried not to see her mother's face as she reached in her wallet for the bill, but even though she covered the photo window, goddamned Tillie's face burned deadly like radium.

Orlando went back to stirring his saucepan of Hormel Chili Without Beans. When it was ready, he crumbled Saltines onto it. He ate a spoonful of chili. "She sounded a little like a hoochie coochie girl." He ate another. "Crazy." A pirate moth orbited and collided, orbited and collided into the bulb above Orlando's crown. Carmen, Carmen, who was this Carmen?

Something had happened to his hunger. He left his bowl of chili on the kitchen table and stepped out of doors. He climbed onto the roof of his panel van. The metal was cool. Club La Comete rotated atop the Regency Hotel like a huge weapon. Whatever this Carmen was—was up there.

He laid down. Carmen. Carmen atop the heart of the city. "Am I suppose to go there or what?" He meditated. Aircraft crisscrossed above. Imagine all the numbers telling each one where to go. How to fall and how to rise. Where do I go? Carmen. What if Carmen was a communist? What if Carmen was bait in an Internal Revenue Service trap?

Orlando fixed his enormous eyes on that trio of stars bright enough to pierce the veil of clouds—stars . . . sleepy stars . . . so much like golf balls glowing underwater in country club ponds.

* * *

Rio Bravo Valley, 1958

Tío Tomás and Tía Chela's shiny blue Ford truck had pulled up to the large clapboard country house where the Palacios clan lived. Bobbstitching chickens, yelping dogs, cats in figure eights, nanny goat with devil eyes chewing on a watermelon rind, cacophony of grackle in adjacent fields, and the thirteen Palacios children, ages 8 to 24, fidgeting and checking their

hair, from very personable to somewhat shy, from quite slen-
der to joyfully chunky, from air of confidence to the mumbled
speech of the lost, the Palacios spilled into the yard to receive
the out-of-towners come from far-off Houston.

Tío Tomás was loud, happy, Indian dark and polished. He
wore Red Wing steel-toe boots and starchy new khaki Dick-
ies, pants and shirt, every day of his life. Tía Chela was a bit
wide in the hips, and she had her outfits. "Spanish blood" fed
her cells. Jet hair, stitched onto white skin powdered even
whiter, framed her face. *Smeraldo e zaffiro* eyeshadow brought
out her hazel eyes. Tía Chela liked brooches: music notes,
starbursts, grapes, a Roman coin, a clock, flowers with rhine-
stone dewdrops, a mandolin, a tightrope artist, a harlequin,
a broken arrow, a dachsund, a merman. She wore a Trojan
horse.

When *tío y tía* pulled up, she waited for one of the boys to
walk up and open the door for her. With a little skewed tilt
of her head, she attempted to cue the Palacios boys, who just
stood there gawking at the jewel of a pickup truck, one of them
combing his greased hair in the Ford's lacquer.

Tía Chela sat waiting in the truck, and still no one reached
for her door. They just stood there like bumpkins, *rancho*. She
rationed her smiles. Her husband was hugging his sister and
pinching her cheeks and looking up at his hometown sky—he
had forgotten all about his *Chela . . . chelis, chelita, chula,
chalupa, chelín, reina de Houston, reina del mundo*. Tía Chela
glared at her nephews. Tía Chela cocked her chin up a notch,
then another. Orlando was the one. It was Orlando who
pushed his way through his brothers and the dogs and the kids
to open Chela's door. He was the one who took Chela's hand
and helped her down onto soil. Only she and Orlando noticed, cared. One brother was hugging Tío Tomás. One of the
teenage girls had climbed onto the bed of the truck and liq-
uidly hula-hooped for the mob. Two other brothers had
popped open the truck's hood and were checking out the
engine.

"Es un V-8."

Tía Chela kissed Orlando on the cheek.

"Es un V-8."

The oil on the dipstick dripped off like honey.

Tía Chela was now moving about. Tia Chela's black and white shoes matched her purse, beautifully, the purse matched her patent leather belt quite well, but Tía Chela's lovely belt with a hint of a fat roll overflowing onto it, did in no way match the shoes. That chink left the aproned, rumpled hostess, la Señora Palacios, a bit more at ease. She'd always contended that Tía Chela was *sangre pesada*. One of the girls served lemonade.

Orlando's papa had gotten the boys to slaughter two kid goats for Tomás and Chela's visit. The goat blood and some of the meat went to make *sangritas*, curdled blood stew, a spicy delicacy in the Río Bravo Valley. After the heads were lopped off, the goats went on a long spit along with fifteen or twenty chickens and a dozen enormous homegrown onions. On that same fire pinto beans seasoned with saltpork and tomatoes and beer simmered in a crock the size of prize-winning pumpkin. A couple of the kids fought over who would get to ride the bicycle, which turned a pair of rollers, which rotated a belt and cranked the spit loaded with the feast. Orlando had designed and built the contraption just the night before.

The skinned goat heads were toyed with for a while, brothers grossing out sisters—that type of thing. After being sprinkled lightly with comino, rubbed very very lightly with cloves of garlic, they were dropped into burlap sacks still fragrant with the smell of onions. The burlap sacks were bundled, tied, and positioned in a pit with stones and mesquite embers. The pit was covered with *nopalitos*, new and bright green prickly pear paddles and mesquite pods, and that layer was covered with more stones and embers. The heads would cook in the earth for eighteen hours.

While the adults were off dancing at the *Baile Grande*, the oldest boys had drunk beer around the fire all night. They talked. They hunted rabbits. They grilled rabbits. They'd go to their sisters' windows, lean there and talk about friends and constellations. In small corn tortillas, the eyes, brains, and tender meat of the goat's head would be had by the adults for breakfast.

Needless to say the food of that visit was exceptional. And after the visiting and the shopping trip to Mexico, and the pious lighting of candles at la *virgencita*'s shrine in San Juan, after the laying of flowers on gravesites, after the passing of gifts (Oldtimer pocket knives for the boys, Max Factor toiletry sets for the girls), after the feasting, storytelling, and laughing, after the kite fights, bingo, and softball, Tío Tomás and Tía Chela drove off the *ranchito* and headed toward Houston. Tía Chela sat in the middle. Tío Tomás hung his arm out the passenger window. The two were very happy. They had never had the blessing of a son or daughter.

Orlando drove the new Ford . . . a great pleasure. Every nut and bolt held at factory specification. Cams, bearings, gears spun and locked smoothly, firmly, into and out of each other. Not a rattle. Not a headache.

As the trio crisscrossed the Río Bravo Valley, Tío Tomás litanized and catalogued the fields worked, crops picked, his sister's cooking, boyhood pranks . . . *pelón pelacas, cuidando las vacas pelón pelacas.* He celebrated the homeland left behind, the home young, quiet Orlando drove himself out of.

* * *

A taxi pulled up to 3412 N. The Battle of San Jacinto Way. A stunning but teetering woman got out. From the trunk, the driver struggled, cussed, but retrieved a vacuum cleaner—a serious self-propelled industrial model made in Switzerland, property of the Regency Hotel & Conference Center.

Charlamaigne dragged her vacuum cleaner across a perfect little duplex lawn. She straightened her dress and dropped the knocker a few times. No answer. She looked in a window.

"The meter's running," the taxilady yelled.

Charlamaigne, feeling like she was going to throw up her Tom Collinses, turned back to the taxi. "Ain't nobody home," she said. The taxilady nodded her head in mock pity, a bit cross-eyed.

Charlamaigne walked back. And the vacuum cleaner was forgotten at the door.

Charlamaigne did not look too good. She had stumbled and tripped twice. And when some big mirror-eyed dog started barking upstairs through an open window, "awoofa awoofa," she really began breaking down. But Charlamaigne wasn't a crier. She was a laugher. She could have the scariest look of dread on her face, but she'd be laughing. Her grandmother had been a laugher, too. Mother Tillie was a crier.

Lit by the beige glow of a neighbor's bathroom light, she saw him. He was laying face up on top of a white commercial van. "We've Got Balls! Reconditioned Golf Balls 24 Hours a day." The van's vanity plates read "Go Golf."

"We've got ta la la la balls" piped into Charlamaigne's head, but who had time for humming radio jingles? It was *him*. His eyes were closed it seemed. His mouth was open. It was him alright, alabaster . . . Spanish dreaming.

Charlamaigne pointed to the sleeping bachelor. The taxi-lady gave her the finger. She was obviously a tomboy.

But she didn't stop with the finger. The darn taxilady retracted into her cab and pulled up behind the van. She flicked her high beams on and off. She began honking the big Checker's horns in very precise three second intervals. Three on, three off.

Charlamaigne's insides came right up with her nervous chuckling. The dog barking had triggered other dogs and some wiseguy not too far off, who was into mimicking catfight noises, stirred the dogs even more.

Atop the van stood Orlando Palacios of the Lord Jesus. He wore boxer shorts and a t-shirt. He pulled one knee forward, obviously trying to cover any delineation of his privates. He rubbed his eyes. And it seemed like forever with the "awoofa, awoofa" and "honk, honk, honk," and the smell of bleach in the air, and the whole neighborhood riled up.

But he smiled.

"May I help you?"

"Why yessir, I'm selling this nice vacuum cleaner here. May I impinge?"

"I mean, it's night, m'am."

"Night is a mood don't you think," Charlamaigne said, impressing herself. She was serious again. She ran her hand from the top of the vacuum cleaner to the bottom and back to the top.

"It's a real nice model, señor," she said. She was good. She twirled her fingers wherever there were chrome curves. "Do you have an outlet?"

"Goddamnit!" The disgusted taxilady helped herself to the fare and a sweet tip. She threw Charlamaigne's purse out and laid a patch as she drove off.

Orlando had gone and changed into pants and a shirt. The frazzled and sleepy Charlamaigne snooped around the spartan but charming apartment. Hundreds of records. Scuba diving equipment. A 2,001 piece tool set. "Old money," she thought.

She demonstrated the vacuum cleaner. It had lights, a forward and a reverse, a little steering wheel, and stirrups where the operator could ride along. It worked miracles.

With perfect posture and a serious far-off gaze, Orlando rode the vacuum cleaner down the hallway, turned around and rode around the sofa thirty maybe forty times.

"I love it," he kept saying. "Does it have attachments?"

"No, no attachments. What you see is what you get."

She sat down on his sofa.

"I'm hungry," she blurted to her Ben Hur.

"I've got chili and eggs. I'll make some."

She kicked her feet up.

"Yes."

"Working late tonight, eh?"

"Yes."

"Never seen a lady selling vacuum cleaners."

"Yeah."

A tear rolled down Orlando's cheek.

"Never seen a salesman in a taxi neither."

He was dicing an onion.

"What's your name miss?"

"My name's Carmen." She was plummeting fast. Spinning sofa. Moths. Johnny Mathis and Orlando Jesús, far-off kites.

"Whoa boy . . . whoa." Orlando stepped out of the kitchen. "You're Carmen?"

Carmen was nodding off.

"How much does this vacuum cost?" She thought she heard him call to her.

"70,000 dollars." She may have said.

Orlando put away the eggs, the Hormel chili, and the Texas toast. He turned down the music.

He emptied a bucket of golf balls and placed it by Carmen's head. He removed her silver shoes. Her big toe nail had come off . . . well, not quite. Like a little desperate man, a shred of flesh retained the nail to the body.

He watched over Carmen. When she vomited, he gently cradled her beehive head. When she slept, he cleaned golf balls one by one as he had done in the first days of We've Got Balls.

. . . I stop to see a weeping willow
cryin' on his pillow
maybe he's crying for me

All seemed right in Houston with the exception of the sales-lady's toe nail dangling, catching on the blanket's fibers. The

Swiss vacuum cleaner came equipped with its own tool kit. It would be okay. That pair of stainless steel college pliers set in blue velvet, strapped in by gray ribbon, would perform the trick, beautiful.

ORLANDO RAMÍREZ

AMERICAN-AMERICAN

I had this conversation with a Eurasian woman
in an Aussie pub in Singapore.

Between sips of vodka and tonic I told her
I'm distrustful of everything and everyone,
particularly the government,
that I want all my information
uncut, unedited, without so-called experts
to tell me what to think.

That's a particularly American attitude, she said.
*Who cares what the government says
so long as everyone is making money?*

"Hold it," I said, "I'm not American-American."

You're as American as they come, she laughed.
*I see them all—The Australians, the Brits,
the Japanese, the Swiss—let me assure you,
you're American-American,*

"But I'm also Mexican."

So? I'm half-Chinese and half-Portuguese.
She took a long sip from her drink then said,
No, I know Mexicans, too.

"But I speak Spanish," I said
as she signaled the Malay waitress
in the Australian football jersey
for another round.

*See? Only Americans make a big deal out of
speaking more than one language*, she said.
I speak English, Malay and Cantonese.

"But you don't understand," I replied.
"The government insists on calling me Hispanic."

*Who cares what the government says?
What does it say on your passport?*

"American."

Listen, she said, pulling me close
to whisper in my ear.
*I know three guys,
one of them in this bar,
who would slit your throat
to sell that on the black market.*

THE WOLF AT HAND

It was not a month
her mother had been murdered
that she answered
an ad in the paper
for a wolf.
That was November
and it rained all month
and when Thanksgiving came

she locked the damned thing
in the garage,
but all through dinner
we could hear the wolf
pace and whine and rip
at her mother's furniture,
so once we finished
she said, *Let the dishes sit*
and we went walking
to the lake.

There had been a freeze,
then a thaw
and what was frozen
clung to the shallow end
where we stood
on the pier listening
to the ice break
in the persistent lapping
of the waves.
The clinking
of all the cubes
in all the glasses
at all the cocktail parties
being held that night
all around the world
could not have matched
that sound of shards sharpening
against water.

I was trying to think
of the right thing to say
when the wolf got impatient
and dragged us

to the parking lot to play.
Watch this, she said
as the wolf disappeared
into the darkness
at the corners of the lot
where lovers had busted
the lights over where
they parked.
Suddenly, the wolf appeared,
all legs,
as if to attack
Don't be afraid, she said,
holding my coat
so I wouldn't step away.
Then she put out her free hand
for the wolf to lick
as it passed.
Now you do it, she said,
and I held out my hand
but at the last second
I made a fist and pulled my fingers away.
*You never know what's
going to happen* I said.

I do, she said. *I know
the stitch that will hold,
the brake that will fail,
which rose will bloom
blood red then pale.
I know which lie
will be false
and which will sound true
once the lawyers
start to argue.*

I know the wind
and the weight it will bear
and how long it will take
to empty an afternoon
of despair.

That wolf was given away.
She left her husband
for a man who beat her.
I left town
and one day
came to my knowledge
when I called the LA sheriff
and asked if a plane
had crashed into
my sister's house
Yes came the reply.
That structure
has been destroyed.

Days like today
when the cold and clouds
lay over the valley like a hand
over a snoring mouth,
I wake from my deliveries
to feel the sandpaper lick
of what I don't know.
Doors open.
Some burn to their hinges.
Cars start.
Others rust through
in a single day.
Everything manmade
comes under suspicion

as the hot breath
on my hand
leaves the flavor
of indecision.

I want to call my old friend
but I don't know what she will say,
Don't make me material
for your poems.
So I greet the wolf
with an open hand,
the soft meat of the palm
a delicacy for him
to want and understand
as I offer this prayer,
Father, Brother Wolf,
whatever name you choose,
please do not betray me,
I am in your care.

A HOUSE AMBIVALENT AS THE SUN

I

Perhaps there is a planet
not tied to a sun
where days might last
32 hours or four,
where they called an end
to the work week
when they had had enough
and on Saturday night

closing time was a buddy,
always ready for another,
and Sunday snapped short
like elastic pants,
leaving TV preachers
just enough time to scream,
Send money or go to hell,
before Sunday night opened its legs,
peeled back its butt
and hung one quick one
before sleep,
decisive sleep,
grabbed us in a headlock
of sweet, brotherly dreams,

2

Just the same, I've accepted
the sun and gravity
and made my way into debt
the way prey follows
the prospect of berries
bursting, pop, pop,
on its tongue
through hedges barbed
with unnatural projections.
I realize that age
makes some men predators
and others scavengers
and of the two
I am of the reluctant kind.
I tell you this
because she says,

I love mating your socks.
Cleaning your lint
from the dryer's screen
makes me whole.
And she gets mad when I reply,
"Right, bitch, and a poem
is supposed to be
an objective experience."

3

In defiance I'd like to turn
myself inside out,
to lay all the parts
of my experience
on the garage floor
and wash each one
lovingly in gasoline,
then leave them there
for her to trip over
on the way to the dryer.
I want her to stumble over
how my father preferred my twin,
how the nuns hated Mexicans,
how I am a big cry baby
when it comes to soggy cereal,
why I long to push my body
beyond time
into the rigorous howling
of matter and subjectivity,
and why I chose this,
a house ambivalent as the sun,
when it comes to my desires.

THIS IS WHERE

I can no longer bring myself
to idealize the purr
of the power mower,
the taste of butane,
the shouts of joy
at an unexpected score
or wail of car alarms
in the undiscovered stillness
of Sunday afternoon.

This is where I spawn,
where the particulars
of my confederation
seek the Spanish syllable
to express the shock
that here,
among the eucalyptus
and satellite dishes,
we are the poetry
of an empire
on the verge of revolt.

In the cities students
spray *Death to Advertising*
on the palace walls,
erect styrofoam godesses
to halt the advance of APCs.
Here we worry about
amortization and escrow
and what women wear on TV.

I am powerless to act
because this is where

the fiction comes to closure,
where the protagonist
refuses to get in his car
and drive away,
where the family goes on
with the barbecue
because it's what
they do every Sunday
and don't know
what else to do.

I'd like to indulge the feeling
that if we are patient
the tempest will skip
this exit,
never make it up
the ramp,
forget to cross the boulevard
and neglect to
make seed of our house.

I know that it happens.
How the world can be
conquered and consumed
in a single afternoon,
leaving just ashes
to pick through
as entertainment
for the camera crews.
This is how it starts.
I know because
it's already here.
I dare not say no.

THE WAY THE WOMEN

Even though
we inherited
our fathers'
faces,
thighs,
hairlines,
senses of humor,
the queer thing emerges
nonetheless
and we photograph
like the old women.

The nanas,
the tías,
the bisabuelas
suddenly take their due
in an expression
on the lips,
the arch of the eyebrow,
the angle of the shoe
crossed at the ankle.

It is beyond being a mask
the way the women
hover through us
like the bleeding
apostrophes of a
Kirlian photograph.

And this is not
meant to be powerlessness,
not unless
you want it to be.

But for me,
and I presume for you, too,
it's the way
the blood says man
and means woman, too.

THE TEST

I hold my palm over the whiting ash.
Before the count of three
my hand feels the heat
and I know the coals are ready.

The chicken goes first,
then the pork ribs
and the Italian sausages.
Through the kitchen window
I hear my friends talk
as they tear at the lettuce,
push the serrated edge
through the tomato
whisk the oil and vinegar.

It occurs to me that this
is what I know of death.
Either you test it or it tests you.
The idea, though, is to get
as close as you dare.
Not that you learn anything
except your tolerance for pain
and that the fire is ready.

The same seems true of love.
We test by waiting
and if the fire doesn't burn
or the wait is not too long
we proceed to this making—
of love, of beds, of payments.

I don't know how I became
so middle class, so available
to these possessions.
Once I had only contempt
for men like me
in shorts and baseball caps
barbecuing in the calm of midsummer.

As I stand alone,
listening to the rasp
of the palms
as pigeons push the fronds
to get at their nests,
I must tell you this—
you will never find anyone
so ready to be put to the test.

IN THE ALLUVIAL

The paleontologist walking
behind the bulldozer
yelled *Stop* and took a stick
to where the backhoe
was about to cut a line

to the city main
and traced the snout
of a dolphin in the dirt.

The site supervisor came running,
bitching because
we're already a week behind,
but the scientist said
this dolphin was a discovery
and started stringing up stakes
and making calls on
his portable telephone.

He says where we build
was once all water,
that floods would wash
camels and pigs and mastodons
into the bay
or dolphins would
sink in the silt
and the sand would salt them down
and leave only the bones.

I couldn't help but picture
a million years from now
when whoever they are
come across these
piece-of-shit houses
we build in the alluvial.

Maybe they'll discover
me and my hammer
and my tin of tobacco
and come to some crazy conclusion
like I was king

and I ruled over a crazy tribe
that did nothing
except drink beer and watch cable TV.

Or else they'll see me
for who I am,
meat from the neck down,
two strong arms and strong back,
a guy who does what he's told
in hopes they leave him alone.

ROBERTA FERNÁNDEZ

Double Talk

I

Aquel jueves todos pronto supieron lo que no debían saber.
Juan Pérez y los otros muchachos se habían ido desde la ma-
drugada cuando primero había corrido la noticia de que pronto
iban a venir por ellos. Por eso, para las tres de la tarde, todo
mundo se encontraba en su casa detrás de puertas bien cerra-
das. Y, a lo lejos, a eso de las cinco, tal como se había anun-
ciado, se veía el jip que ondulaba hacia el pueblo. Sólo doña
Milagros en su casa de tres pisos se atrevía a mirar por la ventana, y desde allá arriba los veía acercarse poco a poco hasta
que el polvo que levantaban oscurecía no sólo lo que dejaban
tras ellos sino aun los borraba por completo.

Doña Milagros ya había visto lo que de nuevo iba a ocurrir.
Desde su ventana lo había atestiguado cantidades de veces.
Gracias a Dios, hasta ahora la patrulla no había encontrado a
los que buscaba. Ni a ninguno de sus parientes tampoco. De
todos modos el pueblo se iba enpequeñeciendo cada vez que
llegaba la patrulla. Algún día hasta ella tendría que mar-
charse. "¿A dónde me iré?" se preguntaba mientras escuchaba
el estruendo al lado de su casa. Era obvio que la patrulla per-
dería paciencia pronto. Hasta ahora, gracias a Dios, no le habían podido hacer daño a nadie y por eso les estaba entrando
una rabia tremenda contra todo el pueblo.

"Tendré que dejar mi casa cuanto antes," se decía doña
Milagros mientras observaba cómo los patrulleros andaban
indagando en tres casas en busca de Juan Pérez. Desde arriba

veía cómo los soldados iban desparramando gasolina por todo la casa que hasta entonces había pertenecido a la familia Pérez. "Vámonos, muchachos," les oyó decir al instante que sintió el ardor de la quemazón de al lado. Tropezándose en las escaleras, doña Milagros rezaba que no se fueran a quemar las otras casas. Y cuando por fin llegó a la calle, los otros vecinos ya andaban echándole tinazos de agua al incendio, y a la distancia, subiendo hacia la montaña el jip iba desapareciendo.

"Ya los muchachos habrán llegado al otro lado de la montaña," cuchichaban los que pronto irían por ese rumbo también.

II

Para su tercer día de fuga, Juan Pérez andaba solo, puesto que los cinco amigos habían decidido separarse para tener más movilidad. Sólo Miguelito se había quedado con él hasta llegar a la frontera con Chiapas. Allí cada uno había hecho la lucha de cruzar la frontera por su cuenta con el intento de reunirse luego en el mercado de San Cristóbal de las Casas. Por dos días Juan Pérez anduvo preguntando cautelosamente por su compañero pero hasta ahora no había dado con Miguelito. Ya para el viernes perdió toda esperanza de encontrarse con él.

"¿Qué te habrán hecho, Miguelito?" sollozaba, "Yo ya no puedo quedarme por aquí. Tendré que tomar el camión rumbo a Oaxaca y de allí, despacito, me iré subiendo a otras tierras. Ojalá me cuide el diosito." El, que nunca en sus quince años había estado fuera de su distrito, se entregó a sus sentimientos. Luego se limpió la cara con la manga de su camisa blanca y se dirigió hacia la estación de camiones.

III

Por varias semanas anduvo en camiones de tercera de pueblo en pueblo, cada vez llegando más a su destinación. Para

ahorrarse sus frijoles y tortillas hacía cualquier trabajo y, hasta
entonces, no había tenido dificultad en encontrarse sus cham-
bitas, pues era un muchacho limpio y trabajador y suficiente-
mente listo para inventarse respuestas apropiadas para las
preguntas que le iban haciendo. Al fulano que quería saber de
dónde venía, Juan Pérez le contestaba que era de Chiapas o
del Yucatán. Pensando que no le convendría decir que era
quiché, se identificaba como maya y decía que su padre le había mandado en busca de un tío que debería andar por esas
partes. Siempre trataba de hablar lo menos posible pues sabía
que los campesinos mexicanos ya habían notado cómo cantidades de su gente iban pasando por esas tierras. No sabía si él
les iba a simpatizar o si le denunciarían. Mejor no arriesgarse.
Mejor quedarse con su soledad que a veces le invadía todito el
cuerpo, haciéndole menos cauteloso. Sin embargo, casi siempre
que iba a extenderse hacia una persona le venía desde muy
adentro el deseo de protegerse. Y entonces volvía a su soledad. No fuera que lo devolvieran a su pueblo donde de segu-
rito le matarían. Y sólo por haberles dado un saco de maíz y
una gallina a dos jóvenes que habían pasado de prisa por allí.
¿Quién iba a decir que ese acto de caridad les iría a condenar
a él y a sus compañeros? No se podía fiar de nadie. Sólo de su
familia y ahora todos estarían desparramados como él en tierras ajenas. Cuando pensaba que quizás nunca más vería a su
mamá, se sentía como una estrella solita en la inmensidad del
cielo a la medianoche. Mejor no pensar más. Una vez que
cruzara la otra frontera comenzaría a darle fuerte al trabajo.
Después de un tiempo quizás ahorraría lo suficiente para
poder volver a su pueblo incógnito a buscar a sus parientes.
Ojalá que en aquel entonces se encontrara con alguien que le
pudiera dar avisos acerca de su familia.

Llegó el día en que Juan Pérez tuvo que dejar de viajar por
camión ya que se le fue poniendo peligroso. Al cruzar de un
estado a otro unos oficiales le habían tomado preso porque no
llevaba ninguna forma de identificación. Pero mientras esos

hombres cotorreaban entre sí, se les pudo zafar y desde ese día, o caminaba o dependía de aventones, lo cual llevaba su riesgo también.

Pero por fin Juan Pérez tuvo suerte. De pura casualidad dio con don Evaristo, un camionero norteño que lo había tratado como hijo y le había prometido llevarlo hasta la frontera y quizás hasta más arriba. De vez en cuando don Evaristo le aconsejaba que se bajara y caminara por varias horas. Después se volvían a encontrar en un lugar señalado por el norteño. Don Evaristo le contaba cómo él había viajado por este mismito rumbo hacía ya cuarenta años. Le había pasado lo de siempre, puesto que el coyote que lo acompañaba le había pillado todo su dinero.

"No quiero que te pase lo mismo," le aseguraba su amigo.

Cuando por fin llegaron a la frontera, don Evaristo le dijo a Juan Pérez que lo llevaría hasta Chicago con tal de que él se cruzara por su cuenta.

"Te esperaré el viernes en la placita de las aguas de color a las diez de la noche. Si no estás allí, yo le seguiré solo."

Entretanto don Evaristo tenía varias cosas que hacer al otro lado.

I

[That Thursday everybody soon found out what they weren't supposed to know. Juan Pérez and the other boys had left at dawn, just as soon as word got round that they'd soon be coming to get them. That's why by three o'clock in the afternoon everybody was at home with the doors locked. And in the distance, round about five, just as they'd said, you could see the jeep snaking its way along the road towards the town. Only Doña Milagros, whose house had three stories, dared look out of the window, and she could see them getting closer and closer until the dust not only left a cloud that hid what was behind them, but also enveloped them.

Doña Milagros had seen it happen before, and it was going

to happen again. From her window she'd seen it often enough already. Thank God, until now the squad hadn't found whoever they were looking for. Nor their relatives either. The town was getting smaller every time the squad came by. She too would have to leave some day. "Where'll I go?" she wondered, listening to the racket next door to her house. It was clear enough that the squad was going to lose its patience soon. Up to now, thank God, they hadn't been able to harm anyone, but that was getting them mad at the whole town.

"I'll have to leave home as soon as possible," Doña Milagros said to herself as she watched the soldiers inquiring at three houses, looking for Juan Pérez. From upstairs she watched the soldiers spreading gasoline about the house that until then had belonged to the Pérez family. "Let's go, boys," she heard them say just as she felt the heat from the fire next door. Stumbling on the steps, Doña Milagros prayed the neighboring houses wouldn't catch fire too. When she finally reached the street, other neighbors were already throwing pails of water on the fire, and the jeep was disappearing in the distance, climbing towards the mountain.

"The boys must have got to the other side of the mountain by now," whispered those who'd soon be taking the same route.

II

By the third day of his flight, Juan Pérez was alone, since the five friends had decided to split up, the better to move around. Only Miguelito had stayed with him until they arrived at the border with Chiapas. There each had struggled to cross the border alone, intending to get together again in the market place at San Cristobal de las Casas. For two days Juan Pérez asked after his companion cautiously but until now hadn't located Miguelito. By Friday he lost all hopes of finding him.

"What'll they have done to you, Miguelito?" he sobbed. "I can't stay around here any longer. I've got to take the bus to

Oaxaca, and from there I'll move along to other places bit by bit. Please God, help me!" In all his fifteen years he'd never been outside the area where he'd lived, and he gave in to his tears. Then he wiped his face on the sleeve of his white shirt and headed for the bus station.

III

For various weeks he travelled from town to town in rickety old buses, getting gradually closer to his destination. He took any job he could find to pay for his beans and tortillas, and it hadn't been too hard to find work, since he was a clean, hard-working boy, smart enough to come up with the right answer when they asked him something. The guy who wanted to know where he came from was told Chiapas or Yucatán. He didn't think he'd better tell them he was a Quiché Indian, so he said he was Mayan and his father'd sent him to look for his uncle, who ought to be around there somewhere. He tried to speak as little as possible, since he knew the Mexican coun-tryfolk had noticed how many of his people were coming through that part of the country. He didn't know if they'd feel friendly towards him or tell the authorities. Better not risk it. Better be alone, even if he felt loneliness overcoming him and making him less careful. Still, when he was going to open up to someone, he nearly always felt the need, deep down inside, to be careful. So he settled for being lonely. They mustn't take him back to his town, where they'd kill him for sure. All he'd done was give a bag of corn and a chicken to two young men who'd gone by in a hurry. Who'd have thought that doing something kind like that'd make him and his friends guilty? You couldn't trust anyone. Only his family, and now they were all scattered like him in foreign parts. When he thought he might never see his mother again, he felt like a star all alone in the midnight sky. Better not think about it any more. Once he'd crossed the other border he'd start working real hard. He might even save up enough after a time to go back to his town secretly and look for his relatives. He hoped he'd still find someone then who could give him news of his family.

The time came when Juan Pérez had to stop taking buses because it was getting too dangerous. When he crossed from one state to another, some officers had picked him up for not having any identification papers. While they were chatting among themselves, he managed to slip away, and from that day on he either walked or depended on lifts, which was risky too.

At last Juan Pérez had a spot of luck. By sheer chance he met up with Don Evaristo, a truck driver from the north who treated him like a son and promised to take him to the border or even further up. From time to time, Don Evaristo advised him to get down and walk for several hours. Then they'd meet again in a place the man from the north had told him. Don Evaristo explained how he'd travelled that same route for forty years now. It was the same old story, the crook who'd been with him had stolen his money.

"I wouldn't like that to happen to you," he told his friend. When they finally reached the border, Don Evaristo told Juan Pérez he'd take him to Chicago, but he'd have to get across the border alone.

"I'll wait for you on Friday in the square with the fountain with the colored lights at ten o'clock. If you're not there, I'll go on alone."

Don Evaristo had a lot of things to do on the other side before then.]

IV

As the men had slowly died off, one by one, the barrios near the international bridge had become home to old women struggling to maintain some peace of mind as crimes, unheard of in the past, suddenly began to proliferate around them. In recent years, an endless flow of transients made their way through the area, and the elderly women soon discovered that their homes had become sitting ducks for the desperate and the needy. With a few exceptions, the women had been living in the neighborhoods all of their lives, but in the last few years, they had been forced to watch their community slowly change as a result of national policies made far away, on both sides of the border.

For a long time the news media had been reporting on the break-ins and thefts, which in the past had been unheard of. Small-time drug kings had bought off everyone they needed to buy off. Lately there had even been reports of murders. Without anyone being able to chronicle just when the change had taken place, the residents in the barrios woke up one day with the realization that they were living in a state of siege.

Doña Flora's misadventure had occurred at about this time. She lived several blocks from the river, where many of the incidents had their start. Hard of hearing, one night she had finally woken up to the persistent barks of the dog and the smell of smoke in the house. The smell frightened her but she became petrified when she sat up and discovered that the chest of drawers on the corner had been emptied out on the floor. In a fearful daze she went to the next room where she found a lamp lying on the floor. There, it was slowly burning a hole on the rug, causing the smell that had finally woken her up. Quickly Doña Flora rushed to get a pitcher of water, and as soon as she was convinced the rug was no longer smoldering, she called the police and her daughter Aurora. Her next call was to Doña Milagros.

Doña Flora's neighbor of recent months, Doña Milagros kept tabs of goings-on in the neighborhood from the third-floor window of her narrow three-room after-thought that had been jammed into the space between two homes to supplement the owner's dwindling income. Doña Milagros had not heard any noise but she quickly came over to offer her support. Everything in the room with the burning rug had been ransacked. Two windows had been broken. Doña Flora's purse had been taken and other inexpensive odds and ends were missing. In the kitchen, the refrigerator had been left wide open and all of the food was gone.

"*Son los ilegales*" ["They're the undocumented"], the police remarked. They did not even bother to take fingerprints, for something similar had happened in every house within a mile radius.

"No point in trying to track anyone down. *Todos van de paso. Cuídese, doña Milagros, no más les falta Usted*" ["They're all passing through. Take care of yourself, Doña Milagros, you're the only one left"] they said as they left without offering Doña Flor the slightest consolation for what had just happened to her.

Doña Flora had lost her husband the previous year, and only recently had she passed from a state of mourning to a newly discovered independence she was beginning to enjoy. But after "the incident" she felt forced to remake her life once again, and for many months she became a prisoner of her circumstances. She refused to leave her house alone at the same time that she was afraid to stay in it by herself. So Aurora and Doña Milagros—in need of friendship herself—took turns staying with her. Some of her close friends also helped out with the grocery shopping and visits to the doctor. They all patiently listened to the details of that terrifying night in Doña Flora's life which she recounted over and over. "*Para desahogarme*" ["To get it all out"], she kept saying even as she put bars on every window and door. Her meager funds were spent on floodlights, new locks and thick curtains which remained drawn all day long.

Her friends told each other tales of incidents they too had experienced. Doña Rosa talked about the time she had returned home after a short trip to Mexico. At that time she had found her home broken into by way of a hole cut through the roof. Another friend told of finding her front door ajar when she came home from church in the early evening. All of her appliances had been taken.

But even in their state of anxiety, they managed to laugh at the story Doña Eloísa told them. She had gotten up in the middle of the night to go to the bathroom, and had surprised a young man of around sixteen trying to hide in the shadows of the hallway.

"*Ay, mi hijito*" ["Oh, son"], she had exclaimed, "*¿cuál de mis nietos eres? No traigo mis lentes y no te veo muy bien*" ["Which of my grandsons are you? I don't have my glasses on and I can't see you very well"]. The young man had willingly played the game and had allowed her to lead him into the kitchen, where without putting on the lights she had prepared a sandwich and milk for him, then escorted him out the door.

"*Buenas noches, huelita*" ["Goodnight, grandma"], he had said as he kissed her on the cheek, then stepped out into the night with several of her valuables in his pocket. "*Dios me libre*" ["May God deliver me"], she had exclaimed as she ran to call the police. The next day she refused to identify the young man after he got caught in another house down the street.

Every day the newspaper added to the elderly ladies' fears. Reports of break-ins and unsolved robberies were spread all over the papers. The articles implied that a plague of *rateros* [burglars] had invaded the town, and that when they got caught, more often by the immigration authorities than by the police, they got what they had coming to them. *Ilegales*. The word alone put fear in the heart of the life-long residents whose shades now tended to remain drawn most of the time.

On the day that Juan Pérez crossed the river on his fifth attempt, the paper had warned against a band of teen-age *Ilegales* who were creating havoc everywhere they appeared. Doña Milagros was reading those reports in the late afternoon of that fateful day. "*Cuídese, ya nomás falta Usted*" kept ringing in her head as she read every line in the entire paper. She then put on the TV and heard more updates about the youthful invaders. By five-thirty, scared out of her wits, she packed a small bag and hurried to Doña Flora's. Later, she realized that in her state of panic she had forgotten to close her door but by then, she was not about to go back there.

V

Desde la esquina donde descansaba, Juan Pérez se sentía confuso por lo que había visto. Allá, por el río, había oído rumores de que solamente viudas ancianas vivían en las casitas contiguas. Y ahora acababa de ver a una anciana salir a tropezones con un maletín. Inmediatamente había reconocido la mirada de temor y por experiencia sabía que la mujer no iba a volver pronto. También notó en seguida que la puerta había quedado abierta. Aún más extraño para él, por un instante pensó que reconocía a la mujer.

"No puede ser. Me estoy imaginando cosas," se dijo al decidirse ir en busca de la placita con las luces de multicolores. Siguiendo las instrucciones de don Evaristo, pronto encontró la fuente, luego, supuestamente distraído, regresó a la casa donde había visto a la mujer que le ligaba a su pueblo.

A la distancia, las campanadas de una iglesia le informaron que eran las seis de la tarde al instante que él sonaba el timbre de la casa estrecha. Como se había imaginado, no vino nadie a contestarle pero otra vez se alejó un poco de la casa. Decidió caminar alrededor de la manzana y al regresar, de nuevo volvió a sonar el timbre. Esta vez decidió entrar. Cerró la puerta y se encontró dentro de una cocina bien ordenadita. En la refrigeradora halló leche y fruta y unos pedazos de pollo.

Mientras comía pensaba en la señora. ¿Por qué saldría de tanta prisa? Tanta gente que él había conocido en su pueblo había salido así. Aún él mismo. "No creo que vuelva pronto," se dijo, "mejor quedarme aquí por unas horas que andar por la calle en donde me pueda encontrar con la migra."

Subió en busca de la recámara y allá, en el tercer piso, la encontró. Inmediatamente se metió debajo de la cama donde la sobrecama que daba al suelo lo cubría por completo. Es-

condidito así, se sentía bien seguro. Boca arriba, recordó todos los lugares en dónde había estado durmiendo por tantos
meses. "Ojalá que no vuelva la señora pronto," pensó segun-
dos antes de quedarse dormido.

[From the corner where he was resting, Juan Pérez felt con-
fused by what he had seen. Over there by the river, he had
heard that only widows lived in the little houses down by the
river. Now he'd just seen an old lady coming out staggering
with a suitcase. He'd seen how frightened she was and knew
from experience she wouldn't be back soon. He saw the door
was still open too. Even stranger, he thought for a minute he
recognized the woman.

"It can't be. I'm seeing things," he said to himself and decided to go look for the square with the fountain with the colored lights. He followed Don Evaristo's instructions and soon
found the fountain, and then, absent-mindedly wandered
back to the house where he'd seen the woman who brought
back his hometown to him.

In the distance the bells of a church were telling him it was
six o'clock in the afternoon as he rang the bell of the narrow
house. Just as he'd thought, nobody answered the door, so he
wandered away a little. He decided to go round the block and
come back, and when he did he rang again. He went in. He
closed the door and found inside a neat little kitchen. In the
refrigerator there was milk and fruit and some pieces of
chicken. While he ate he thought about the lady. Why had
she hurried off in that way? So many people that he'd known
in his town had left like that. He had too. "I don't think she'll
be back," he said to himself, "I might as well stay here for a
few hours instead of wandering in the street where I might
run into one of the immigration officers."

He went up to the bedroom and found it on the third story.
He got under the bed, where the coverlet hung down to the
floor and hid him completely. He felt quite safe hiding there.
Lying on his back he remembered all the places he'd slept for

so many months. "I do hope the lady doesn't come back soon," he thought, just before he fell asleep.]

VI

Después de haber estado durmiendo por varias horas, oyó las voces. Sacó la cabeza para escucharlas mejor y vio que el reloj marcaba las nueve. Por unos momentos no entendía lo que pasaba. A lo lejos, en el primer piso, los pasos eran demasiado fuertes. No podrían ser los de la viejita. De repente sintió que las voces venían del cuarto del segundo piso.

"Vamos a llevarnos la tele y el tocadiscos."

Alguien hablaba en tono natural.

"Yo bajo uno y tú el otro. Pero primero sube a ver qué hay arriba."

Juan Pérez no veía nada pero sabía que alguien estaba abriendo cajones y vaciándolos en el suelo.

"No hay nada de valor aquí. Pero, ¿nos llevamos la radio y el teléfono?" la voz cercana preguntaba al que obviamente estaba en cargo.

"Traítelos, con toi el cordón del teléfono."

Deslizándose de debajo de la cama, Juan Pérez sorprendió al joven, dándole fuerte con una lámpara de bronce que estaba en la mesita de noche. En seguida tomó la almohada y la puso sobre la boca del joven para que no se oyera su exclamación.

"¿Qué te pasa, cuate?" gritó el otro al sentir el ruido que hizo el cuerpo al caer al suelo. Juan Pérez veía que el que estaba inconsciente era un muchacho que parecía ser más joven que él.

Instintivamente se acordó de las tablas que soportaban el colchón, las cuales había estado mirando desde su lugar en el suelo. Rápidamente jaló el colchón a un lado, tomó una tabla y esperó detrás de la puerta. Cuando el otro muchacho subió, Juan Pérez le dio con todas sus fuerzas contra el estómago, luego le pegó en las sentaderas, y finalmente con cuidado le dio en la cabeza. Al ver que los dos jóvenes estaban inconscientes, se dio cuenta de que tenía que salir al instante. Dejó todo tal como estaba y se fue corriendo hacia la placita de las luces de muchos colores.

[After sleeping several hours, he heard voices. He stuck out his head to hear them better and saw it was nine o'clock. For a few moments he didn't understand what had happened. In the distance, on the first floor, there were heavy footsteps. It couldn't be the old lady. He suddenly heard the voices on the second floor.

"We'll take the TV and the record player."

Someone was talking in a normal tone of voice.

"I'll take one down, you take the other. But first, go upstairs and see what there is up there."

Juan Pérez could see nothing, but he knew they were opening drawers and emptying the contents on the floor.

"Nothing of any value here. How about the radio and the phone?" the voice close by was asking someone who was evidently in charge.

"Bring 'em along, the phone cord too."

Slipping out from under the bed, Juan Pérez was upon the young man, he hit him with the bronze lamp on the night table. Then he put the pillow over the young man's mouth to muffle his cries.

"What's going on, brother?" called the other on hearing the noise of the body hitting the floor. Juan Pérez saw that the boy who was unconscious seemed even younger than himself.

Instinctively he remembered the boards holding the mattress, he'd been looking at them from his hiding place on the floor. He pulled the mattress quickly to one side, took a board and waited behind the door. When the other boy came up, Juan Pérez rammed him as hard as he could in the stomach and then hit him on the behind and finally on the head, but carefully. After making sure the two boys were unconscious he realized he'd better get out immediately. He left everything the way it was and ran towards the square with the fountain with the colored lights.]

VII

In the house next door, the dog barked incessantly. The two women peeked through Doña Flora's front window at the exact moment that the door slammed behind Juan Pérez. *"Parece que anda alguien en su casa"* ["It looks like someone is in your house"], Doña Flora said as she rushed to the telephone. As she had done so many times in her imagination, she pushed the number she had programmed in for speed-calling the police, then the one for the immigration office. Within three minutes the familiar pale-green car from immigration screeched to a stop in front of her house. Ten minutes later, the police car drove up. By then the first officers had found the wounded boys and had radioed for an ambulance.

"Looks like gang members fought against each other in your house," they told Doña Milagros, who was moaning softly as she followed instructions and looked around to see what was missing.

"No falta nada" ["Nothing's missing"], she told the police, *"excepto mi ánimo de vivir. No se pueden imaginar lo que he pasado para llegar aquí, ¿Y de qué sirvió todo eso?"* ["Except my will to live. You can't imagine what I've gone through up to this point. And what was the point of all of that?"]

By the time the ambulance arrived, the two boys had regained consciousness but neither could describe what had happened. *"No vimos a nadien. Tal vez hay fantasmas en esta casa"* ["We didn't see anyone. Maybe there are ghosts in this house"].

Doña Milagros sobbed uncontrollably. *"No se asuste"* ["Don't be frightened"], Doña Flora whispered, stroking her neighbor's face. *"Podría haber sido peor. Tal vez le han hecho provecho los rosarios que hemos estado rezando durante estos días"* ["It could have been worse. Maybe all the rosaries we've been saying lately helped"].

VIII

Mientras Juan Pérez iba corriendo hacia la placita con las luces de multicolores, las campanas sonaron la hora. A la distancia veía el camión de don Evaristo pero no sabía si éste le había visto. Ya que iba acercándose al camión vio que las luces se prendían y luego se apagaban y entendió que su compadre le estaba dando una señal. Al abrir la puerta del camión ni siquiera saludó a don Evaristo. "Arránquese. 'Horita le voy a contar lo que ha pasado."

Al terminar con su historia, Juan Pérez por fin se dio cuenta de que estaba temblando.

"Hijo, eres un héroe. Lástima que no lo vaya a saber nadie. Pero Dios te lo pagará más adelante."

Y salieron, rumbo a Chicago.

[While Juan Pérez was running towards the square with the colored lights, the bells were chiming the hour. He could see Don Evaristo's truck in the distance but didn't know if he'd seen him. As he got closer he could see the lights go on and then off again, and understood his friend was signalling to him. As he opened the door of the truck he didn't even greet Don Evaristo. "Start up. I'll tell you what happened."

It was only when he finished his story that Juan Pérez realized he was trembling.

"You're a real hero, kid. Trouble is, nobody'll know. God'll remember though. You'll get your reward."

And they set off for Chicago.]

IX

The next day the newspaper ran a front-page article on the break-in with its strange extenuating circumstances. The two men, it reported, had been released from the hospital and were locked up in the local jail. From the appearance of the house it seemed that the gang of illegal hoodlums had started a gang war, making them more unpredictable and more dangerous than before. The news was repeated hourly on the TV and the radio, and the elderly women called each other up to check on the latest developments. Doña Milagros, it was rumored, had been admitted to the hospital and had sworn she was going to keep moving farther north.

Pobrecita. Que tenga que empezar de nuevo otra vez. Y a su edad" ["Poor thing having to start over, and at her age"].

No one went to visit her at the hospital though, for the other residents in the neighborhood were too frightened to leave their home. None went out that day nor the day after. Instead, they all stayed home and waited for the special bulletins which appeared on their radios and televisions at a steady and mesmerizing pace several times throughout that day, and every day from then on. The announcers promised that the *ilegales* responsible for the misery in the barrios sooner or later would indeed get what they had coming to them—a one-way passage back to where they belonged. To reassure the audience that the authorities meant business, they even flashed three or four pictures of those recently rounded up. Doña Flora and her friends gasped as they saw Doña Milagro's face for an instant on their screen.

In answer to their frantic calls, they were told that Doña Milagros had already been sent back home. *"Cuídense de personas como ella"* ["Be careful around people like her"], they were warned. Doña Milagros had gotten off very easily, for there was a good reason why her home had been ransacked. Several small plastic bags with white powder had been found under her bed, but the authorities had decided that because of her age, they would simply send her back home.

"Remember," Doña Flora and her friends heard a voice say, "nowadays, there's no one you can really trust around here. *Cuídense. Cuídense"* ["Be careful. Be careful."]

Note: Translations are by Alita Kelley.

PATRICIA BLANCO

AND SO ON

After a long period of doubt
maybe a grudge is lifted
and you pursue small things
and things you can read about,
a well-considered day,
a brief brush with proportion.
This is all about faith,
which is grief, twice reflected upon.
And then you make up your mind
it's the work you have to do,
the making of space, and so on.
And isn't there relief in losing
what you love most, a way of floating
to earth without noticing your death
seeing all manner of things sprung up meantime
and everything saying yes.

TWO REFRAINS

I

And your love, so docile and arbitrary,
like everything else.
And since it's like everything
you have to make certain judgments. The day—

that's enough. I've always said that, haven't I?
The day, that seeps through every morning
leaking its casual fire,
which you accept on its own terms, or maybe
some other terms but that gets burned away
sometime later. To think of it later—that's the only time
you love anything.
But try now: to see, to walk,
the bounce of consciousness, a context
too arbitrary to dwell on, like my first
breakthrough, the ache for someone,
the way absence survives.

II

It was strange that the smell of lemon cake
should travel that far
and the bowl of oranges' bouquet—
my winter was transfigured by these,
the clock's inwardness, simple tools,
and it includes a mystery.

The nights we need
work upon us
like an excellent transformation:
like any simple thing
we sit around in April, past midnight,
the trees are swelling,
soon you'll be gone, so we don't need any
better reason: we sit, say few things,
the star jasmine is beginning to flower.
It will be heavy this year.

SONG

I'm speaking of that
time just before
spring, say,
the very day
before. The night air cold
but sympathetic. You
might have been with
other strange girls
and suffering
the monotonous languor
of fifteen and all you cared
nothing about—
only this moment:
to be awakened
to the fact of your
body, vague
aching, alert
to romance, etc.,
and later, its replacements.

IF MY GRANDMOTHER AND I WERE CONTEMPORARIES, SISTERS

She would have recounted to me
stories she'd read as we stood side by side
at the sink washing dishes.
She would have read in the back bathroom
Friday nights to cry freely
at "The Scarlet Ibis,"

that explosion of color,
pride a *wonderful, terrible thing*
bearing two vines, life and death. . . .
I want to know how far
such a night would travel through her
keeping her from the real-life choices
which could all the while be swelling inside her
like underground streams determined to flood.
And I imagine she grows distracted anyway,
mid-adolescence, to wed Andrés at fifteen
he appearing not in Jalisco
but Phoenix, Arizona, 1970,
dark and thick with his impossible serenade
and I notice her face
not indignant but falling,
a face I never knew.
If Mondays we'd taken the bus
to piano lessons downtown,
it might have been enough,
the wandering indecision of *Sarabande*, off somehow,
maybe just that fraction of door ajar
to expose everything she'd need to know
for her for some time.

SOLDIERS

are in the kitchen,
their blown-out faces
in the regulation helmets.
They're stuffing their faces with bread
and cake.

they've got their
overcoats on
and their chapped hands
upon the bread.

One is machine-gunning
the pot on the stove.

PHONE CALL TO CUBA

I. Jewels

When we were kids my sister broke
a thermometer and cupped a perfect bead
of mercury in her hand, rolling it back and forth
for me to see, the eerie silver concentration of it,
the danger of it I already knew and I imagined how easy
to lick it up off her hand and faint quickly away,
the way I wanted.
One day Rosalía cut herself while she was
taking care of us and forced her Indian blood
out hard and it was a red darker than mine,
a richness almost mud.

II. Will

Once, I swam out into the wide spoon of the ocean
very far, past where the pompadour hairstyles
of the waves rise. I was singing inside the story
of a woman's journey alone. With each
verse I plunged out farther and farther,
exhilarated by the sun baking my face, the thick,
salty coldness taking my body. When I turned

to go back, the tide resisted, and continued to take me
out to sea, as if to say the choice were irrevocable. I
   fought hard
against the sucking mouth of it and then went under
once or twice, gulping in water, the electric fear
tasting like childhood. I wanted to live.
Some distance away, several people
stood at the far end of a pier, looking far off
at the horizon. Some would listlessly raise an arm to indicate
a point of significance and then turn away, unconvinced. I
   heard
the light bells of their voices and I called out to them
but they couldn't hear. Later, I lay on the shore,
rescued, motionless, an infant, letting the life
seep back into my altered body.

III. Phone Call to Cuba

At this point I dread to be told what I already know.
A woman ringing the same number again and again.
At this point I possess very few enigmas: residue of foreign
   memories,
a phone call to Cuba, the potential
for mediocrity. But it wasn't always so—at seventeen,
I followed the endless, stiff-backed tidings
of socialist meetings, opened books with the religious hush
like the beginning of love; the lust
to prove my existence. Now, only the profile remains:
love and will, my proximity
to rebellion.

And it's just the cruel choice. It's just the merciless choice.

DEL ALBA

The sky almost aqua with dawn,
where black velvet
becomes mohair, and then chiffon,
and at the waistline of the horizon,
a studded netting
of late stars fizzing and popping

far above the orange trees and
their Indian feet.
With the dawn you think of
young girls and their stupidity,
their lightheadedness,
their silver mouths held open a fraction too long.

THERE WERE DAYS

The pleasure was fresh days
we cracked open
and between them, you,
a joy as athletic
as any after-school at twelve.
And I wouldn't have turned back
if the view weren't breathtaking
and didn't you prefer panorama
though later lost interest in travel
and lost what converts
the noon of every ordinary day
to redeem it in dusk?
Maybe it's enough just to know it's there
though you will never go back

only keep records of the temperate places
and the way it went up
stylish and pastel
as a young breeze.
But if you can say it
with any conviction
remember *there were days*
when the immeasurable blue
transcended my demands
for a clear sky
and remember
the rewards of earnest damage
and the world that turns
continually to another sun.

SKETCH

The painful, exquisite bite of lime
from our parents' daiquiris.
Our parents' parties—all mood
and explosion. Mona dancing,
pulling a shawl back and forth
across her behind to a rumba
or cha-cha. Later she would be crying
when someone insists on playing
Las golondrinas or *Solamente una vez*,
songs she requested at her father's funeral
so that she could cry all the harder.
My mother's wide smile—
red lips and perfect teeth.

Everything is lime green and
crimsons of the coastal town
we came from.

LA EDUCACIÓN

There was a way of saying it
that meant you were going to get out.
The myth of our chicana daughters
who turned their chins to college;
sober, determined, but swelled anyway
at twenty-five with children and mechanic husbands . . . .
I never knew them really, nor understood;
they were one wave before me,
in the sixties, with boyfriends
who went to war unaware and well-meaning.
Those daughters who majored in business
or education, who brushed out the faces
of their parents' lives into a blandness
that impressed everyone:
rows and rows of subdivision
curling around the edges of town.
But what of that?
Maybe it's only their tastelessness I resent still,
their future with no point of view,
the limp in their English;
so long in school and still that inflection
that corrals you: minority.
My sister and I withdrew by other routes,
lining up off center,

following paths of pure fancy
through a door we liked to call Art,
so alien or neutral it evaded talk
amongst our relatives of success or failure
and took on a life of its own
that could only be judged *movement*.
And I'm only too glad to find the path
insistently turns, turns always sharper,
yielding a language more and more precise
but with color and background,
the whole breath of what I remember,
and so escaping with it in the hope
I emerge everything: daughter, myth, chicana.

THE MANGO'S CORE

Flat, white, and dangerous.
A furry clove. Everywhere on the ground,
eaten and abandoned,
in Mexico.

You must do everything
in the peach-orange fruit;
all that was *worth* two months
in the green.

ROLANDO HINOJOSA

A Spring Break

This selection is an excerpt from *The Useless Servants*, a novel in progress. The work concerns events and characters during the Korean War. Because it is a work in progress, a few explanations concerning the abbreviations used are in order:

NKPA, the North Korean People's Army

CCF, the Chinese Communist Forces

Glosters, a unit of the British Brigade fighting in Korea

Intel/Recon, the Intelligence/Reconnaissance personnel

HE, Heavy Explosive charges

Forward ob. Forward observer in an artillery unit

SCR-300, at times a highly unreliable radio used for troop communications

The title "The Useless Servants" comes from the Roman Catholic Mass, Luke 17:10; this writer uses that version. The Protestant version calls them *the unprofitable servants*; the writer feels this is a poor rendition of the original writing by the Apostle.

March 17, 1951. Got back from the hospital in time for another attempt to retake Seoul. As usual, we wait for a big supply build-up. And, in the meantime, the CCF is engaging the US Army and taking big losses, but all the time making us pay, too. As usual, when the CCF stops fighting, it stops, flat out. They move out of an area and go off to reorganize. They probe some, but mainly they pull back. This is now a usual tactic, and it doesn't mean anything other than they may be short of food, shoes, and other equipment. It doesn't mean they're through fighting.

Still no word on Charlie; he may be a POW, and if so, let's hope it's CCF.

March 18. Our unit crossed the River Han; we're in the out-skirts of Seoul. I'd not noticed just how big a city it was; although now it's mostly leveled (our arty and CCF's). No refugees to impede our crossing this morning, but they'll be back now that we've crossed the Han and they think it's safe to be back in Seoul. They'll show up soon enough.

Intel/Recon guys stopped by our unit and gave us the word. Be very careful in dealing with refugees; there may be NKPA among them. GIS warned to be prepared to shoot. (How can we tell who's who? Great advice: use your best judgment).

March 19. The refugees streamed in this morning. We had no trouble with them. The Han is still very, very cold, so the refugees had to be patient, although many chose to go right on in. What a place to come home to. Our patrols say that the Chosen Hotel is a heap of cement and said the same thing about the Bento Hotel.

(These refugees are the poorest of the poor). Everything they own is on their backs. Everybody—kids included—carry a load. Their shoes are a mess, and then there's that ice. Jesus.

We are still bringing in much equipment across, but as soon as another bridge goes up, the refugees start using that one, too.

News: Gen. Ridgeway's liaison plane landed not 1500 ft. from us. He's still visiting as many units as possible. So, it's back to "Tent City" for HQ and the Os when he comes in.

Rested a pad on a tailgate and worked on old firing charts from the first time we passed through Seoul. No idea if we're going north again and no idea if CCF is going to push us south again. It's said that Old Guys and Os have no news as to CCF strength and to expect more hard fighting ahead as a consequence.

But, Ridgeway is patient; a patient killer, and we've killed thousands by arty alone; no telling what air and ground attacks have done, but I can imagine.

Wrote home. Still no word on Charlie here. Expecting the worst. Got Joey on the radio, and he's coming over tomorrow.

Hat. and Frazier came by: how's the eye, how's Tokyo, and

how the hell are you? Was told that Dumas, Stang, and Skinner were in a back area for two—three days. On their return,
Hat. and Frazier will get some days off, too. I'm to get two
new gun crews to break in, and we'll see, after that.

Played cutthroat pinochle with Brom and Ichabod and then
to the sack.

March 20. The Inf. is at work again and the Intel/Recon guys
go out early. Intel/Recon units carry much firepower for a pla-
toon: five Jeeps (two with M-guns and three with SCR-300 radios; two tanks; a mortar section; and some Inf. to accom-
pany tanks.

All reports from runners say the same thing: CCF probing se-
riously and patrolling aggressively to see what we've got, and
then our guys go out to see what they've got. The Air Force
has a difficult time spotting CCF. It's been this way most of
the war.

CCF are a tough bunch of people. Os say they're far away
from their supply bases but that they are still being supplied.
Our Air Force will shoot at anything that moves: trucks,
trains, etc., but CCF is still being supplied because they also
use men and animals for transport.

The Air Force is still a danger for us. It's frustratingly difficult to coordinate with ground troops, and so the AF will acci-
dentally fire on our troops. Not long ago, when we had the
Glosters fighting alongside, the AF shot at them by mistake. No
idea how many were killed, but a good bunch is the word.
No idea how this was resolved.

This is how it happened: Things got pretty screwed up in
the Pass last November, and the ridges were mobbed with US
Army and CCF troops and much firing all around by our Inf.
and us. The Gloster arty had cleaned off a hill of CCF and
then, suddenly, our Air Force came roaring in and caught
the Glosters on open ground, high on a ridge. There wasn't a
place for the Glosters to run; they were pinned like flies, and
they died the same way.

At first, the Glosters must have looked up, probably relaxed their guard at the sight of our Air Force, and then had no chance to react. Many were hit and killed.

March 22–24. Acc. to runners leaving area, there are some good-sized patrols on both sides, and they keep running into each other. Lt. Brodkey has registered on everything we have up front. We also have good communication with the Signal Corps wire strung up, but the CCF must be creeping in at night since the Signal guys have to replace the wire each morning.

The Listening posts have been set up below the Forward Ob sites. The CCF patrols at night, too, but there's no set schedule for them. And, the listening posts report movement in the areas where our GIS are not sent, so it must be CCF. And, we can't fire since this can lead to all manner of foul-ups, so there it stands.

News regarding Seoul is that most of our troops have crossed the Han in good order.

Dumas, Stang, and Skinner are back, and out went Hook and Hatalski for a few days rest. Dumas talked about the Pass and the Chongchong to the three of us. Skinner asked about POWS, and Dumas said that in combat it's best to disarm and abandon them. They become too much trouble to feed and lug around, etc. And NKPA, I asked? The Germans and the Japs also murdered GIS, he said. I mentioned the SS reputation, but Dumas (he was in Belgium for a while) said that regular German army units also shot POWS outright.

He said that the Pass was typical: roadblocks, rivers to cross, night fighting, etc. POWS are in the way of both sides; this is one reason why American POWS have been released, and why we release CCF POWS at times. Of course, he said, and this may have also happened at the Pass. The same POWS may be recaptured later and held a second time if CCF held that ground securely. This happened at the Pass since we got in our trucks and were moved to safety.

Dumas then asked if I've taken any pictures. Told him I'd

forgotten my camera, that it was probably among some of the equipment I left in my old barracks bag. Stang then said that much of that stuff is rotting somewhere in the port of Pusan. That's God's truth.

We went back to POWS for a while, and I said I'd not heard of our side shooting POWS. Dumas said we probably had, but that the US Army is hell on that, and that a guilty GI would be tried in a flash. That's the way it works, is what he said.

Dumas made it official; I'm in charge of my old gun crew again, and that Stang and Skinner are to work with me.

We heard some small arms fire, but it was far away and not aimed in our direction.

March 23. Joey came by and brought beer. He's worried about Charlie, and I told him of Dumas's talk on POWS. I said Charlie was probably back in some field hospital getting patched up and that we just had not heard of it. Sometime back, the battery clerk had said Charlie was still being carried as missing for now. We were on this when two trucks came in with new guys for our outfit, and who comes in but Sonny Ruíz!

He'd been in Pusan most of the time and missed the Pass but was in on the Feb. 17 offensive and the drive north to here. Typical Ruíz luck: wounded twice, lightly, on both arms and hip, but perfectly okay now, he says. More like a burn. Shrapnel of course. He was standing behind the gun and shielded from the blast, but he still caught two finger-nail sized pieces of NKPA or CCF HE. He was patched up fast, went to a field hosp. for two days, and with no infections reported, he waited two more days until he found transport to rejoin his unit.

Brought news from Japan; he'll marry that Japanese school-teacher. No plans after that except to retain his US citizenship if he decides to stay in Japan. Says his Mom taken care of by Chano's WWII insurance and Social Security which is still more money than she ever earned working as a maid for the Logans, the Paxtons, and the Ripleys. (It was Sonny who had them take out her Social Security deduction, malgre lui, is how Sonny put it).

He also said Capt. Bracken and Lt. Merritt came to Korea four months ago. Sonny served with Lt. M. and ran a crew for him. Bracken is still a pain, acc. to Sonny.

Received a letter from Klail City relatives of his who wrote him that I'd lost an eye, that people were saying I was going blind. Sonny then laughed and said that Brother William had been right about some of us going blind.

Sonny then asked about Hiro Watanabe and the money, and Joey told him that Hiro was doing okay and that the money was still in the Nippon Bank and at the Tokyo whorehouse. Sonny said we need to give power of attorney to old Yoshiko Ogura in case something happens to us. Good idea.

Joey then told him Charlie was missing since fighting at the Pass. Said he heard about the Pass and asked if people were exaggerating about the fighting there. Joey said the Pass was plenty scary.

After this, we went to his crew; not one guy in it was from the Kwansai District. Sonny says all the units were bled little by little and sent to Pusan until new units were formed. He asked about Hat. Dumas, and Frazier, etc. We told him Lt. Edwards may be dead, but we'd not heard a word on him. Told him we'd lost any number of GIs and Os; none he'd known, though.

Sonny said he'd trained the guys he brought with him, and then Joey filled him in on the unit, and we drank a couple of beers and then Joey went back to his outfit. Sonny then introduced me to some of the guys in his crew; they said they were all squared away, and Sonny told them he'd check with the Sergeant (Dumas) about where to sack out, etc. Told him I had the duty that night, and that tomorrow he'd met the other guys, Brom, Ichabod, etc.

March 24. At 0700 hrs. three liaison planes buzzed by on their way north. After early chow, we worked on the guns. Two new guys for us came in yesterday with Sonny Ruíz's crew:

Belton, Harry J., and Cox, Russell K. (both Californians).
They've had some training but have seen no combat, and so
Stang, Skinner, and I put them through their paces to see how
well they work with our system.

Lt. Waller showed Capt. Bracken around, and we showed
him what we could do. The crews worked out okay. Acc. to
Dumas, this is Bracken's first line assignment. Enough said.

March 25. Got permission from Lt. Vitetoe to go see Sonny
and spent half the morning catching up on more news.

S. described part of his arty unit's doings in this past offensive. They were under orders to fire like hell and told there
was no need to advance. They moved around in trucks with
the Air Force spotting ccf patrols and Sonny's unit pouring it
on. Moved north, but slowly. Told him that was smart. "Look
at us," I said. "We got caught in the Pass and paid for it."
Etc. etc.

Ate with Sonny and returned to unit. Our Inf. guard volun-
teering to go on Recon patrols. (Bored stiff here and going
crazy. Works out well for all since they relieve the regular
patrols).

The day dragged by; I couldn't even read since everything
was so dull around here. Asked Dumas if there was something
we could do, and he said to go see Lt. Brodkey. This got me
out of the area and took a funny book with me, *The Zebra
Derby*; it's about post-wwII vets.

Ross, one of Brodkey's crew of runners, considers himself a
Socialist and said that that type of book is neither serious nor
of any use to me. That's an old argument between us, and I
usually avoid Ross; if he'd ever gone through rank racial dis-
crimination in Texas, then, I once told him, then, you could
talk to me about brotherhood. This time I asked him if he'd
read *Manhattan Transfer*, and he came up with that jargon of
his: that Dos Passos despite his brand of Socialism was not a
Socialist, that he still had some "residual ideology" and so on
and so on. He said my turning my back on Catholicism wasn't

going to save me. I agreed, but I also told him that reading Max Shulman, whom he mistook for some Socialist and not the author of *Zebra Derby*, was good enough for me. As usual, I swore to avoid him in the future, and I'm sure he did the same in my regard. We'll probably all get killed here anyway, for all the good his theories are going to do him. He's smart, though, but he's as stubborn as any Marxist I ever ran across.

Got to the Forward ob. holes (which aren't holes or deep ones either). They usually sit on some hillside with a good view. Lt. Brodkey, Crazy, and Ichabod are adept at arm and hand signals, and have developed a good system between them.

This afternoon, during my visit with them, Brom told how Lts. Bricketto and John died. The two SCR-300s crapped out early during the fight. Two telephone lines were working okay for a while, but since we were wheeling the guns around to fire here and there and back again, both Lts. got up to give arm and hand signals. And then, since each one fell like a stone, right on the spot, Brom, and later Lt. Brodkey figured that'd been picked off by sniper sharpshooters. I've no idea when they were picked up and brought back to base camp. It had been a long, intense day of fighting with much movement in and around our area that I must have missed their being transported by the trucks carrying the dead.

So, I screwed off all afternoon and finished the book. I left it with Ichabod who reads some.

March 27. USO troupes were landed some 15 mi. south of Seoul. That must be a secured area if those people are that close to us. Bracken ordered two truckloads to take in the show. Escaped that and then Sonny came over and he and I got together with the Old Guys.

Lt. Waller came by and asked about the news guys and their training. Coming along is what the Old Guys said. (Lt. Waller looks better; looked terrible in Jan. and Feb.). Still no news on Lt. Edwards. Lt. Merritt came by to check the shell inventory, and he and I went to see Lt. Brodkey. (I called Crazy on the field phone to let him know we were coming down; Crazy spoke like Cary Grant and Jimmy Stewart. Ichabod laughing in the background).

Got to the hill and Crazy waited until Lt. Merritt left with Brodkey, and then Crazy did a Clark Gable imitation. Asked him when he learned to do those voices, and he said he'd been doing it since his voice changed.

Dumped some beer cans in his hole and drank a couple with Ichabod spelling him on the binocs. Crazy tells the worst jokes in the world, but he's good at his job. Ichabod is a good partner says Crazy; trouble is Ichabod can go days without saying a word. Brom says Ichabod is part Trappist; Ichabod had no idea what that meant.

I asked Brom if he were Cath. and said yes. From this to Cath. Schools, catechism, serving at mass, etc. He went to a Jesuit school. Told him of Marist Bros., but he said the Marists are tame when compared to the Jesuits. He called the Jebbies the Gestapo of the Catholic Church.

This is the first long talk with Bromley; his first name is Billy, not Bill or Wm. He's from Muncie, Indiana; he wants to be an actor, and he wants to be rich.

Back to base camp with Lt. Merritt (talked about his twin sister; a spastic, he called her—don't know what that means). Lt. M. went to a private school in South Carolina. Asked me if I planned to return to college. Sure, if we live through this.

He reported to Capt. Bracken, and I then went to the hot water barrel and dropped in two cans of hamburger patties.

We still had two hours of daylight when the gun crews returned from the USO show. We then listened to a lecture by Intel/Recon guys: there's increased night precautions, and they take effect tonight since the CCF is getting bolder.

Asked Joey about the USO shows; a piece of shit, acc. to him and to everybody else.

(Before hitting the sack, Hat. and Frazier were driven in. First thing that damned Capt. Bracken told Hat. was for me to be issued a US Army fatigue cap, right away, and to stop wearing the cap I got from Boers, the Marine. I asked Hat. if I'm to pay for the cap and Hat., smiling, said: "Well, it'll probably be deducted in your next pay period."

One of the bothers with no fighting going on in the area is that Os get chickenshit since they've little else to do.

As Joey usually says: "It's different with Bracken; he's one of ours, he's a Texan."

March 28. Surprise orders this morning after early chow. Two gun crews (mine and Skinner's) were trucked to a back area and from there to an assembly point. Looks like the fighting will be on us soon. Got me a soft cap and loaded up with C-rations. Kept the usmc cap since I'll be out of Bracken's sight for a while.

DAN COOPER ALARCÓN

Shortchanged

I'm just about to shortchange the guy when someone shoves a photo under the glass.

"Seen him?"

I glance up. It's a lady cop: stocky, short hair, her face pudgy and sweaty, her dark-blue uniform almost comical on such a hot day. I look back down and say, "No," as I slide the correct change to the other side.

"Why don't you look at it first, wise guy?" she says.

The line to get into the fair is growing, people are getting impatient and the small ticket booth is baking in the sun.

"I said I haven't seen him."

As I slide the photo back to her I look at it. It's a kid, a boy, maybe six or seven, tops. He's got brown hair with straight bangs—what we used to call a Tupperware buzz when I was that age—and one of those wide, unself-conscious, little-kid grins.

She takes the photo and puts her face up close. God, you're ugly, I think, and I'm glad the thick glass separates us.

"Try a little harder," she says. "He was last seen here on Sunday."

Today's Tuesday.

"Lady, 20,000 people come through here every day and half of them are kids—there's no way I'm going to remember one."

"Thanks for nothing," she says and swaggers away.

I go back to selling tickets. I feel bad but what can I do? Parents should keep an eye on their kids. I look again at the long line and the ones on either side and feel dizzy. It's all pastels, loud shorts and too-cool sunglasses. Behind me, the rides are screeching and kids are screaming.

"Christ," I mutter and concentrate on shortchanging the people. I make more that way than I do from the $3.25 an hour they pay us temporaries. I've been working the state fair every summer since I was fifteen. Selling tix isn't bad, just real boring at times, but you can make good coin if you know how to shortchange: "walks" we call them. The booth gets hot as hell though and sometimes it's embarrassing when some of the guys I graduated with last May come through. They always ask where I'm going to college and I get tired of lying. Truth is I won't be going. I'd like to study art, but Dad says hell with that, there's no money in that. Says if I want to be an artist I should go to the Tech and learn drafting, become an architect. It just wouldn't work though—I've never been any good at staying within the lines. Dad'll be disappointed, I suppose, just like Karen was. She's been acting so goddamn weird ever since I told her I'd be working at the mill this fall. Never calls. Never meets me after work. I guess I know what's happening, but lately I've been too tired to want to do anything about it.

The lady buying tickets from me is distracted by her kids. I count to five out loud but I only slide across four singles. She thanks me and pockets the bills without ever looking at them. I'm really getting back in the groove when Rain shows up. Her real name's Rainbow but everybody calls her Rain. Every summer she hangs around my booth—probably because I put up with her, but right now I'm not in the mood.

She raps on the door and I say, "Not now, Rain," before I remember she can't hear me. She raps again and I look at her and shake my head, then forming my words carefully I say, "No—Can't—Busy." It's hard to guess how much she gets, but I'm pretty sure she understands no.

She's shaking her short blonde hair wildly and making fishtail motions with her hand.

"No," I say again.

Now this skinny, long-necked guy with a bad case of acne starts rapping on the window. "Hey," he says. "I've been waiting fifteen minutes."

"Okay, okay," I say and peel off the tickets.

All of a sudden I hear a woman gasp and people starting to laugh. I look up and can't believe it. Rain is dancing around without her goddamn shirt on! Of course, people are staring. How many folks are used to seeing a ten-year-old girl with tattoos all over her body? She's jumping up and down, tracing and retracing her finger over the snake on her chest, its head and forked tongue rising up out of where her cleavage will be if she ever grows any tits.

"Jesus H. Christ," I say and lock the cash drawer. There's a collective groan as I put up the THIS BOOTH CLOSED sign and go outside. I grab Rain by the wrist and try to pull her shirt back over her, but she's twisting around too much and I only manage to get it over her head. Finally, I give up and start to lead her away to find Sandy. The shirt is flopping on her back like a cape and the people in line are yelling after us.

"I'm on my break!" I yell back.

The fair is crowded, but it feels good to be out of that oven. The air is heavy with the smell of popcorn and sweat and manure from the 4-H area. Rain and I walk down the midway, past the tented games, toward the rides. People stare as we pass. I stare at her, too, and I think for a moment how she's really quite beautiful: an explosion of color, a garden with roses and daffodils blooming in the small of her back, a Monarch butterfly perched on her skinny right shoulder blade. The snake's tail starts back here and coils about her twice before slithering up her chest. I think how maybe they should've named her Eve and how no one will ever know for sure what her real name is, because her Ma died soon after she was born and Sandy said her old man, one of the fair roustabouts, got knocked crazy four years later when a tent pole came down in a storm. That's when he started tattooing her and calling her Rainbow. He died two years later and Sandy began looking after her. Sandy says she's never said or heard a word in her life.

We keep walking along the midway, baseballs whumping into sackcloths pegged tight on either side of us and then the rides spread out before us, the Ferris wheel set behind Sandy's carousel like the cogs of a giant clock, the polished steel blinding in the afternoon sun. I start to head for the carousel, but Rain pulls the other way. By the stubborn look on her face I know it will be a struggle to resist, so I go with her. I watch her dirty bare feet pad softly along the littered, sun-baked blacktop—they are calloused so thickly the heat can't hurt them anymore. She leads me to the west edge of the fairgrounds, where the last old ride, a rickety Tilt-A-Whirl, sags like an antique. It's one of McWhirter's rides, that bastard; all of his machines are like him: old and mean. When they run, they wheeze and cough and spew thick black smoke into the air. I'm glad to see McWhirter's not around and that the ride is down. Once I watched him run a ride an extra five minutes because he knew one of the kids was sick and he pretended he didn't hear the kid begging him to stop. I watched him smile as the poor little bastard staggered off and puked his guts out while the planet did loop-de-loops around him.

Rain is tugging at me and pointing excitedly at something in the grass. Then she points at herself. I kneel down and take a close look, but all I see is long grass and the thick black and silver cables that are the arteries of the sick carnival ride.

"There's nothing here, Rain." Sometimes I forget she can't hear me and then have to find some other way to communicate. But come to think of it, I sort of enjoy talking to her; it's kind of comfortable, like thinking out loud. Now I look at her and shake my head no, but before I can stand up one of the clumps of grass comes alive and slithers forward and she grabs my arm.

"Aw, Rain—it's just a garter snake. You almost got me fired because of a garter snake?"

I watch the small, thin snake work its way forward. It reaches the cables and there is a prolonged chatter of raw energy; the snake thrashes wildly, held in the current of enough electricity to turn 2,000 pounds of rusted metal. When it falls still, smoke rises from the blackened husk, carrying toward us the smell of burned flesh. Rain is clawing at me, her mouth open—it is her way of screaming. I force my right hand over her eyes and turn her around, then lean forward. At least six inches of the cable are exposed to the bare wires. I hold Rain's face steady in both hands and say slowly, "It's all right, Rain. It's all right," but who knows if she understands? The snake on her small chest spooks me, and I work her arms through the shirt sleeves. She doesn't resist this time.

I take her hand but when she realizes I mean to take her away she sets her feet stubbornly, so I scoop her up. She's very light for a ten-year-old, and it doesn't take me long to reach the carousel. I ask the carny running it where Sandy is.

"Over by the toolshed," he says. "Some kid got sick."

At the toolshed it's dark inside and when my eyes adjust, Sandy's helping a little boy hike his pants up. The kid is crying.

"Sandy?"

Sandy kind of jumps, then says, "That you, Ben? Hold on. Okay son, you're all right now."

The kid pulls loose and runs past us, away from the rides.

"Poor little guy got so scared on the Ferris wheel he wet his pants," Sandy says.

I laugh. I like Sandy. His real name is Jack Sanderson and he's been a carny all his life. He's tall and thin with sleepy eyes, a shock of thick red hair, and his clothes always look too big for him, especially the baseball shirts he wears every day. Today it's a Royals uniform, but I'll bet he's got one for every big league club. When he talks baseball he gets so excited he reminds me of a little kid, and I think that enthusiasm is what makes him so good with children. When Rain's father kicked off he sort of adopted her.

"It's a little early to be on your break isn't it?" he says casually.

"Yeah, I left on account of Rain. She's a little shook up."

Rain is standing behind me, peeping around at Sandy.

"There's a problem with one of McWhirter's rides," I say. "The old Tilt-A-Whirl on the edge of the fairgrounds. Bare wires. We just watched a garter snake fry . . ."

Sandy looks at me kind of funny.

"I'm not kidding," I say.

He shakes his head. "I'll talk to him," he says. "I'll make sure the power gets turned off. Thanks for looking after her."

He stretches out his hand, but Rain won't let go of my leg. I peel her hand away and I'm surprised by the strength in her skinny arms. I give her hand to Sandy and watch them walk away, Rain dragging her heels and looking after me, moving her lips soundlessly.

* * *

It's a long walk home, but the evening breeze is cool and the wide sidewalks and streets a release after the claustrophobic ticket booth. I'm thirsty and go into Sharrett's and buy a six-pack of Miller. Nick likes me and sells me all the beer I want. Back outside, a convertible whizzes down the avenue, a group of girls inside, their hair and laughter streaming behind them. I miss Karen and walk to her house, but the lights are off and even her parents are gone. That's okay. It's kind of nice sitting on her stoop in the cool dark, their cats rubbing against my legs. After a couple beers, though, it gets real lonely and I start to wonder who she's with, then decide I'd rather not know. I get up and start for home, leaving the six empty bottles carefully lined up on her porch.

* * *

I stand for a moment watching Mom's silhouette move past the kitchen shade. I'm trying to figure how to get in without her noticing—but it feels like one of those hopeless algebra problems they expect you to solve in school. While I'm standing there somebody grabs my arm and I jump about five feet. It's Dad. He raises his finger to his lips and leads me to the garage. Inside, the smell of gasoline, oil and musty cobwebs hit me hard. My head swims in booze and familiarity: the old wooden ladder secured on the far wall, the sandy oil-dry spread out to sop up the leak from the old Catalina that Dad refuses to sell. He leans against it while I rest against his work table.

"How was work?" he asks.

"Long and hot. I'm bushed."

"Your mother will have a fit if she sees you like this."

"Is it so obvious?"

"To her it would be," he says. I don't say anything and he looks away and plays with the side-view mirror. After awhile he asks me to open his toolbox.

"What?"

"My toolbox. Open it."

I flip open the lid of the big gray Craftsman and watch the three inner trays slide smoothly toward me on their terraced rollers. All the tools are neatly arranged, wrenches and nuts on one tray, screwdrivers and screws in another, hammer and nails on the third, pliers, awls—everything there looks brand new. Below the trays is a storage area with some oily rags, a ballpeen hammer and, in one of the back corners, a baseball.

I reach in and pick it up. The stitching has come loose and the coarse cover flops in my hand.

"That's the same one you pitched through the window twelve years ago."

He's right. I was playing catch with Steve and a throw went wild and smashed in the side window of the garage, showering Dad with shards of glass while he sat at his worktable. He stood up and looked through the broken window at us and asked who threw it. Neither one of us said anything, but he could tell just by looking and called me over. Terrified, I walked from the bright hot sunlight into the musty darkness of the garage. When my eyes adjusted I could see there was a cut on his forehead. He told me to take off my shoes and even though he didn't raise his voice I could tell he was drunk.

"Dad, it was an accident," I said.

"Take off your shoes," he said again. Too scared not to obey, I kicked off my shoes.

"Now your socks," he said.

My baseball glove still on, I pulled them off with my free hand. The cement floor was gritty and cold and I kept shifting my weight from foot to foot.

"Now walk over to the sawhorse and bend over it."

I took a step forward, then stopped. The narrow passage between the car and the workbench was sprinkled with slivers of glass. At the other end of the garage, Dad loomed over the sawhorse.

"It was an accident," I said again, starting to cry.

"Your accident almost put out my eye. Now, come over here."

"Ben, I want you to go in the house. Right now."

We both looked around and saw Mom standing at the entrance to the garage. She looked past me at Dad and they glared at each other. Without taking her eyes from him, she said, "Go on. Get in the house. Your father and I have something to discuss."

I ran to the house and locked myself in my room. Steve was already there, as scared as I was. Whatever they had to discuss didn't take long. Five minutes later I heard Mom on the phone and an hour after that Uncle Mal came over and took the three of us to his house. We were there about a week and then came back home, and it was like nothing had happened. The window had been replaced and Dad started going to

AA meetings every Thursday night. Nobody ever spoke about the incident.

"I remember," I say, tossing the old baseball in my hand. I can't figure out if he's apologizing or lecturing me.

"I used to keep a pint where that ball was."

"I know, Dad, but that was a long time ago."

"Yeah, a long time ago."

He seems surprised that I knew and I almost feel sorry for him. We both look down at our feet and are quiet until the silence becomes uncomfortable.

"Seen today's paper?" he asks.

I shake my head and he motions to the newspaper on the workbench.

It's on the front page, bottom right. Headline: HAVE YOU SEEN HIM? The text gets all jumbled by the alcohol but the photo connects. It's the same one, same stupid haircut, same silly grin.

"Poor kid," Dad says. "The parents must be out of their minds."

I'm so tired I can't respond, just nod my head. Dad's small hands are stroking the cold-faded blue of the Pontiac and I have this feeling that something unusual is going to happen. Next thing I know, I'm talking to him about Rain, but I'm too drunk to tell it well—she comes off sounding like a sideshow attraction.

"She's got nobody," I say. "If she got lost, nobody would care. Just me and Sandy."

"Hell, Ben, she wouldn't be happy anywhere else. Those carnies live in a different world."

He walks to the garage door and looks at the house. "Wait here five minutes and I'll get your Mom into another room. And Ben—go easy on that shit from now on."

Before I can say anything, he's inside the house. I squeeze the ball tightly for a few seconds and then carefully put it back in the corner of the toolbox and close the lid.

* * *

It's almost noon when I haul my butt down to the kitchen the next day. Mom is standing with her back to me, slicing tomatoes. She says, "Good morning," without turning around, and I know her choice of words is a kindness.

"Morning," I mumble, squinting at her.

Her hair is pulled back and in the hard flat light coming through the window I'm surprised by how old she looks, and I wonder how I haven't noticed before. As she slides the tomatoes away and begins to peel an onion I see that her pale blue work shirt is stained beneath the armpits.

"When did you get home last night?"

"Late," I say. "I stayed to have a couple of beers at the fair."

She doesn't say anything and I hope it's because she appreciates the grain of honesty in the lie.

The aroma of the over-ripe onion fills the room and she begins to tear up. She turns on the tap and rinses her hands, but the water dies to a dribble. "I've got to get a plumber over here. Don't get mixed up with those carnies, Ben."

"I'm not." I can feel myself getting mad, but what's the point in saying anything? I want to tell her they're good people. If they shortchange a customer now and then it's only because they don't make a decent wage.

"There's fresh oj in the fridge. You'd better have some before your brother gets home from practice."

"There's always fresh oj in the fridge," I say, feeling my hangover shift into high gear. I resent this room and its orderliness: its neat spice rack, the telephone with its "Have a Nice Day" memo pad, the big round clock over the sink. Even the spotless walls lob their yellow light at me, lodging it behind my eyes where it beats painfully. I close them and hear Mom slicing expertly through the onion, the knife making regular, staccato contact with the cutting board. The noise stops and Mom is saying, " . . . it makes sense. You're talented and it's what you like to do."

I open my eyes and stare at her.

She grabs a handful of mushrooms and washes them quickly in the initial burst of water.

"Ever since you were a little boy you drew on every scrap of paper you could find and when there wasn't any paper you'd start on the walls. You probably don't remember your Zeraffe, do you?" she asks.

"Zeraffe?"

"We had just put up some new wallpaper in the nursery, really bright and cheerful with a floral pattern that turned that room into a garden. A couple of days later you got loose in there with your crayons and drew a giraffe among the flowers, a giraffe with black and white stripes. It was pretty good for a five-year-old."

"Yeah, I remember now. A zeraffe. I remember the paper, too. Whatever happened to it?"

"Oh, you just kept marking the walls up until we finally decided it would be cheaper to take the paper down and paint over the walls every year. Anyway," she says, setting the knife aside, "I'm going to talk to your Dad about art school."

I don't know what to say.

"Well, you'd better get moving," she says, "or you'll be late for work."

"Yeah, okay." At the door I pause but she's gone back to slicing.

* * *

The next day I have a surprise for Rain. On my break I take her away from the fairgrounds to an embankment overlooking a large construction site. The machines are far below us and look like toys, the men eating their lunches like specks. We sit down and I give Rain half of the sandwich I bought along the midway and one of the two Pepsis. The sun is brilliant and the heat seems almost to have weight, pressing down on us. I guzzle the Pepsi and strip off my singlet, mopping down. Rain takes off her T-shirt and I blink at the colors that blossom next to me.

"I can't blame you, Rain. No reason you shouldn't when no one's around."

She eats, never taking those big eyes off me. It's kind of spooky. I look at her and I think of mermaids and angels.

"Your old man must've been something, Rain. Wish I could've met him," I mumble into my sandwich. I look at her again and those dark eyes bore into me and I have to look away.

When she's done eating, I lead her by the hand farther down the embankment. It levels off into a weedy field and I hoist Rain up onto my shoulders so that she won't be cut by any of the burrs. She starts clapping her hands and I tighten my grip around her legs and break into a trot. The heat wears me out in a hurry though, and as soon as we're out of the field I kneel down and let her clamber off. She's smiling at me and clapping her hands.

"Maybe I should hire myself out as a carnival ride," I say. It makes me feel good to see her so happy.

We keep walking over to an expanse of recently laid cement that looks like the foundation of a new building. At the far end of this is my surprise for her, but before we're even halfway there, Rain tugs on my arm and points to two footprints in the cement, one smaller than hers, the other an adult's.

"We used to do that when I was a kid."

I run my foot into the depression of the larger print. There's a good half-inch to spare all the way around and a distinct tread, kind of like the clubs on a playing card.

"Guess some guys never outgrow it," I say. "C'mon, I want to show you something." I take her hand again and walk her down to the other end where early this morning I drew a picture for her in colored chalk: it's the garden her tattoos make me think of. The scene is simple and stylized, filled with patches of color that create the illusion of lush green vegetation and brilliant flowers. Over them hovers a cluster of gold markings that suggests butterflies. There's also a Zeraffe towering over some red trees, and peeking out from behind one of them is a smiling face. Underneath the cement square I've written RAIN in big blue letters.

"That's you, Rain," I say slowly, making sure I have her attention. I touch her and then touch the face in the drawing. "You—Rain."

When she realizes what I mean, her face contorts just the way it did when we saw the snake electrocuted. She jumps forward, scrubbing at the face with her hand. I can't believe it, and for a moment all I do is stand there stupidly and watch her rub furiously at my drawing. When I grab her arm and pull her back, I see that her palm is lacerated, streaked with red chalk that looks dull next to the shiny droplets of blood. The face in the drawing is completely blurred, just a mass of color blending in so well to the rest of the picture, you can't tell there was anyone there.

"Jesus, Rain," I say, looking at her hand again. I take out my handkerchief and wrap it around the palm, knotting it in place. I can feel her body heaving with rapid breaths, her face tense and grim. I try not to feel hurt, try to concentrate on helping her put her shirt on, but all I see are those tattoos running together into a chaotic mess. Despite my will, I remember how excited I was this morning, how my hands trembled as I opened the brand new box of chalk, not because it had been so long since I'd drawn anything, but because it was for Rain and I didn't want to fuck it up. I remember kneeling, then lying on the concrete, still cool in the early morning, feeling the chalk collect in my pores and nails, the delicate moment before I laid on any color. I remember hoisting that first green line, the chalk snapping under too much pressure. I picked up one of the halves and tried again, this time with more of a sense of the texture and how soon everything else just fell away and there was only my hand, the chalk and the color pouring from it.

"Sorry you didn't like it," I say and force myself to take her good hand in mine. I look across the weedy field and beaten-down snow fence and see Sandy silhouetted against the heat haze. I wave but he doesn't wave back. I shrug and lift her onto my shoulders and start back across the field toward the swaying ferris wheel.

* * *

Friday morning it rains early but stops by the time I get to the parking lot. Today's the last day of the fair. Today I get paid. I say hello to Rick, one of the other ticket sellers.

"Did you hear about the retard?" he asks.

"What?"

"You know, that tattooed retard always hanging around here."

"What do you mean? What happened?"

"Take it easy, man," he says, knocking my hands away. "They found her in back of McWhirter's ride about half an hour ago. The paramedics and cops are there now. What a mess!"

I push him aside and run down the midway and the ground seems to cave inward, slanting up around me in high walls. I feel like there's a rock or something stuck in my throat. The police and ambulance lights strobe red across the tents as I get close. The fair hasn't officially opened yet, so it's just cops and workers. I slip under the police line and I'm headed for the covered stretcher in the ambulance when someone grabs me.

"You don't want to see her," Sandy says. "She's dead."

"Rain!"

He nods, grimacing like he's grinding his teeth. "She must have come back looking for that snake."

"But McWhirter was supposed to turn the power off!"

"I watched him turn it off myself, Ben. Nobody knows how it got turned back on."

"Rain!"

I'm looking down at the ground, not really hearing what Sandy's saying. He's tracing circles in the dirt with the toe of his big workboot. I stare at the worn treads and the studs on the sole of the boot. He grabs my shoulders.

"Go home, Ben," he says. "Collect your pay and go home."

I turn away and look at the paramedic securing the ambulance doors. A police officer comes over to us.

"This is a restricted area."

"Sorry, officer," Sandy says. "C'mon, Ben."

He puts his arm around me and walks me over to the carousel where he slumps down on the metal platform. He takes out a pack of cigarettes and offers it to me, but I just stare at him. He takes out his lighter, but his hands are shaking too much to get the cigarette lit. He tosses the pack away.

"It was time to quit anyway."

"Sandy—you know Rain wouldn't have gone near that ride after seeing what happened to the snake."

"I know. I can't believe it."

"She can't be dead. They must have forgotten something."

I run a few paces before I see that the ambulance is gone. When I look back at Sandy he's standing inside the control booth at the center of the merry-go-round. There's a low hum and the carousel starts to vibrate and rotate slowly, gradually picking up speed. He steps up onto the revolving platform and grabs hold of one of the long poles that support the carousel's horses, swans and unicorns while I stand there watching him spin in and out of view, and I think maybe the whole world's gone crazy.

*   *   *

Dad and I are sitting at the kitchen table. He's been listening to me talk for the last forty minutes. Now neither of us says anything for awhile. At last he leans back in his chair and says, "Do you want to come with me to Jack's for a fish fry?"

Despite myself, I laugh. "I'm not very hungry right now," I say.

"Ben, Rain's dead. That's terrible and it never should have

happened, but it did. She's dead. You're alive. And to stay alive you have to eat."

I look at him and notice how tired he is. He manages a smile. "C'mon," he says, "What do you say?"

I'm still not hungry, but I don't want him to leave me alone.

"All right," I say. "I'll go."

Jack's is a small tavern. It has a horseshoe bar, a few booths on the side and a dart board in the back. It's smoky and crowded. Everybody's just got paid and is noisy and happy. I've got a wad of four hundred dollars in my pocket. I sit next to Dad at the counter over a steaming, heaped plate of food with a beer in front of me, but I'm just not hungry or thirsty, and the smell of alcohol and smoke makes me feel kind of sick.

"Feel better?" Dad asks.

I shake my head. "I should've made her understand that she wasn't to go back there. I should've made it clear. If she just could've understood me better, you know? I was never sure if she understood me."

He keeps eating and says, "You know, I was thinking we could find a way to send you to a college—give the art thing a try. See if that's really what you want."

"Jesus, Dad." I stare at him in disbelief. "Rain is dead and you sit there with your ice water proudly on display and act as though nothing has happened."

People are staring at us so I shut up and look down at my plate. We sit quietly for what seems like a long time and my mind jumps spastically from place to place. I think about how after Sandy climbed onto the merry-go-round, I walked all the way over to the construction site, unzipped my pants and pissed on the drawing. I wanted to watch that stupid little picture bleed in the hot piss, but I couldn't even do that right: some substance in the chalk made the piss run right off.

"Ben."

"Don't say anything."

He carefully places his fork on the plate and says, "We lost a child once, your mother and I. Between you and Steve. A miscarriage."

"I don't want to hear this."

"We both took it hard, but especially your Mom. She was counting on a girl and even made me put up special paper in the nursery. She loved that wallpaper. Always talked about how it would cheer up the baby."

"About a week after the miscarriage I came home and found all of the paper torn off the walls, every bit of it, ripped to shreds."

"How come you've never told me this before?"

"Your mother's ashamed."

"Ashamed?"

"She's convinced she did something wrong. She thinks she could have prevented it somehow."

"That's ridiculous."

"Yes—it is."

He stares at me to make sure I get the point.

"I hate you, I really fucking hate you right now," I say and stand up. "I'll wait for you in the car."

"Ben, wait . . . "

But I'm already outside, the screen door slamming behind me. A couple of steps later I'm bent over double. When I finish retching, I lean back against the building and for the first time I start to feel better. Here it's dark and warm and breezy, and the fresh air helps clear my head. Jack's sits close to the river and there are no streetlights. The only light comes from a phone booth across the road where someone has left the door shut. Mosquitoes swarm around it, trying to get in, attracted by the light. I shut my eyes. The crickets are noisy tonight. Or maybe it's just because there are fewer sounds to mask them. I tilt my head back and open my eyes. There seem to be more stars than usual and they look brighter, too. They circle in the sky like the Ferris wheel at night when it's lit up. It makes me dizzy and I look away, across the river into the blackness and think how right about now Sandy and the other carnies are packing up the fair, how in the morning the only sign that it was ever there will be the flattened brown grass and litter. It's hard to believe that all of those rides, games, people, will be gone—a collapsible city packed up and carted off like a piece of luggage.

All of a sudden I feel like hell again and I wish Dad would hurry up. Down the road I can just make out Olson Construction, where the dark, pot-bellied cement mixers hunker on the ground like sleeping elephants. I stare at the phone booth and then walk toward it, across the gravel parking lot and dirt road, avoiding the shallow pools of mud with crusty footprints in them. Inside, I put in a quarter and call Karen, but the harsh busy signal fills the booth methodically, relentlessly. I hang up and the quarter rattles noisily down the coin return. Through the dirty flecked glass I can see the big sign above Jack's, painted like the Jack of Hearts, and at last I understand.

For my next call, no quarter is necessary.

ODILIA GALVÁN RODRÍGUEZ

CONSTITUTIONAL REMEDIES

me curastes de susto
con escoba nueva
hierbabuena
manzanilla,
y un rezo antiguo

and that mal ojo
que me dio la vecina
boiled to a close
in a glass of water
under my bed
y cuando I fell asleep
to a vela on the dresser
and a picture of Saint Jude
the bad luck was sequestered
by the light of a new moon
pero comadre, me parece que
in the healing ceremony
you forgot to choose
the right remedy to alleviate
my colonization blues

DIOSA

a galaxy of bright stars
adorned her swaying
black night skirt
with silvery threads
of moonlight
sister spiders
embroidered lightening bolt
and web patterns
on the summer sky blue huipil
she wore
a garland of jet snakes
dancing about her neck and chest
radiant face of a billion lives
enclosing eyes of fire and ice
full oxidite lips which broke
into abalone teeth smiles
from time to time
hair the color and smell of wood pitch
from which all life flowed
crowning her head a hoop of white roses
reminding her that she was the queen of the
universe

at first her planet
was cold and still
then she learned that with steps
her feet would make
small impressions on the surface
she could create
blue oceans, rushing rivers
streams or emerald lakes

crystalline water liquid stars
all this made her happy

at the planet her breath
she'd blow
from this tall green
grasses, lush prairies
marshes began
to grow
this gift of life she'd known
now she was generating existence
all on her own
this made her happy

in clay
the same copper color
as her skin
with outstretched
arms and hands
into her world
she'd sculpt
deep canyons,
mighty mountains,
mesas and hills

at night she'd dream the flowers
delicate orchids
snowy larkspur, freesia,
indian pipe, lupine,
calla and tiger lilies,
marigolds, desert sunflowers
bathing in their fragrance
slowly she'd awaken
with ample bouquets
clutched to her breasts

years passed
her home had grown
she traveled from
the jeweled jungles and rain forests
to the ochre deserts and jade valleys
all teeming with her luscious fruits
yet she sensed something was missing
all that lived and breathed on her world
only moved in the winds and rains she'd bring
she wanted beings like herself to laugh and sing

with
Diosa had created a world full of life
but now try as she might she could not find
a way to create an end to her loneliness
one day as she wept
a serpent from the necklace she wore
bathed in her tears awoke and slid away
the little snake could not believe her good fortune
she crawled and marveled
at the world around her
happy to have such a wondrous existence

as serpent slid about she realized
that one day soon she would become a mother
sister spiders came down from the heavens
suspended from silvery threads
they wrapped the mother serpent in a soft cocoon
in the velvety womb new life was being formed
in seven days the silky shell began to give way
from its opening came forth a column of deafening
    wind
a crack of lightening and clap of thunder in the

blue-black sky
in the gales magnificent winged struggled to fly
on the ground in the rain turtles, lizards,
and other crawlers scurried for new cover
there were majestic four-legged insects of every
   kind
Diosa saw everything but could not believe her eyes
she sang a song of thanks and praise
to her new relatives
that night she dreamt of exquisite beings
like those she'd never seen
two-legged like herself and though they couldn't   fly
they could think and speak, laugh, sing and cry
when she awoke lying next to her she found two
   babies
swaddled in the satiny leaves of one of her giant
   trees

SNAKE WOMEN
   to Marilyn

how luxuriatingly
they recline in their
proud multicoloredness
some in skin tight
iridescent garments
others in silk and cotton
robes flowing like
ribbons in the wind
their bodies
oh what bodies

big hipped and legged
firm roundness
strong
shoulders and backs
shapely succulent breasts
givers of life nectar
inviting arms and hands
outstretched in prayer

sitting in a circle
in council
women speak
in dream words
define their lives
their present
their future
they talk of telling
children
the teaching tales
the dream stories
of other years
they chant sing
in full bodied voices
filling up the universe
all living cells
all of the senses
singing
they recite
of all
that has died

of how death
transforms into
all that flourishes
new in the wide world

they grow and change
shedding old skins
with loving compassion
guiding the way
moon is their time piece
from opaqueness
comes the sliver
the half opened eye
to pregnant rounded
brilliance filling up
the sky
like the ocean
their bodies
giving way
open
to
radiant
spilling
life blood
together
their bodies
bringing in
the ever changing tides

BIRTHING

for Alison

woman
whole
within
herself
midwife
to her spirit
she swaddles
herself
in the deep
red darkness
of earths womb
wrapped snug
in a mantle of darkness
lying on rich damp dirt
she dreams
herself
emerges new
and shining
into the world
once again

MARY HELEN PONCE

On Writing

What motivates me to write is MEMORY. *La memoria*. Memories of family, home, church, school, muddy streets. *Happiness*. To recapture on paper images entrenched in my mind, sounds, colors, voices. I inherited my father's good memory and can still recall childhood smells, songs, trees, dogs, books, friends. I never had to invent a happy childhood. I recall the blue dress worn on my first day of school and the blue ribbon atop my Shirley Temple curls. The green grass of *el llano*, the open field we cut across, the kindergarten teacher, principal, and the tall eucalyptus trees that towered above Pacoima Elementary School, are still fresh in my mind.

"Memory," claims N. Scott Momaday, American Indian writer of the Southwest, "is a burden." I agree. Memories can be painful. When my mother was pregnant with me, my older sister Rosalia was dying. While in the womb I absorbed all the sadness and often think of myself as somewhat melancholy. I evolved in a womb of tears, those of my tired mother whose first child was about to die. Unborn children are affected by a mother's mental condition by osmosis. I am certain I absorbed my mother's pain. I am also certain that I can exhume that pain by writing.

I grew up writing. On dirt, fences, rocks, trees, (using a nail) and with my brother Joey watching, scratched my name on a cement wall made by our father. Mostly though, I scribbled on dirt. A favorite thing was to rake a section of dirt, water it down, then when dry, draw figures—or words—with a stick. To this day I collect *palitos*.

I like the feel of a pencil in my hand. Also pen or crayon.
I could have been an artist. As a child I liked to draw my
environment and sketch houses, trees, and the ruffled dresses
I yearned to have, but for the most part painted flowers. I
memorized the shape of daisies, zinnias, calla lilies, and the
tall stalks of my favorite ranunculus, and drew them from
memory. At one time I took up pastels. Using oatmeal paper
I sketched flowers in a wicker basket, daisies in a field, and
stately gladiolus. My sister, an artist, tells me that with practice—and art lessons—I could be a good artist. But when
would I write?

I write because I LOVE WORDS. I keep a dictionary close by,
not to check my spelling (I was always a good speller), but to
learn new words, new meanings to old words, and feel them
roll—or stick—to my tongue. I write because my father, who
taught himself to read both Spanish and English, drove five
miles to buy *La Opinión*, a Spanish newspaper, and by doing
so taught me the importance of words—and how they can
color a world. I write for him.

Words have always fascinated me. As a child, learning the
alphabet was a challenge. Using the Palmer Method, I wrote
my ABCs on a tablet until they looked perfect. In cursive writing my letters were too fat and lumpy, but when I printed,
the letters looked straight, bold, important! Much later I
learned to print block letters, and to this day, I print everything except my name. Letters, class notes, bills.

When writing, I prefer to use black ink. India ink, although
impractical, is a favorite. Blue ink appears insipid, weak. Red
is for correcting papers and labeling fragile packages. I once
taught myself calligraphy. The feel of quill on paper, the
curves and lines of dark letters on white was almost intoxi-
cating. Often nothing excites me more than a clean sheet of
paper waiting for the pen.

I write in my head. I have never kept notebooks for refer-
ence as to plot, dialogue, or Lord forbid, metaphors. In fact,
I disdain the overuse of metaphors but prefer to develop my

own, those mutually exclusive to the story I am telling—or do without. I would rather wrack my brain for something original than borrow from a master writer like Saul Bellow (whose metaphors fit my stories to a T). I admire Amy Tany because her metaphors and similes flow from the story. Nothing awkward there. I avoid clichés and phrases that are trite, cutesy. My goal as a writer is to develop original characters, plots, themes, and when possible, language.

I write best in English. By the time I came along, our family, like most first generations, was quite assimilated. Everyone spoke English, except for my parents and our adopted grandmother Doña Luisa, who spoke Spanish. My father stumbled over English words like "sixty" (pronounced six ess tee), but stood tall when reciting Spanish poems during *las fiestas patrias*.

English was the language of education, of knowledge, and my first written language. English was the language of playmates, except during street games, when we yelled in Spanish. Our one bookcase held Book-of-the-Month literary selections (subscribed to by my sister Cora) all written in English. English was the language of authority.

I rarely write in Spanish, yet Spanish words float in and out of my subconscious. Spanish was the language of family, home, love. *El barrio*. A language spoken correctly by my parents and our neighbors, all Mexican immigrants. Spanish predominated in the *jamaicas*, church bazaars held each summer. We were scolded *en español* and sung to sleep to Spanish lullabies. Spanish was that secret language spoken in Mexican movies shown in San Fernando; the language of sensuous music: bolero, paso doble, tango, bolero-son, vals, and later, the mambo and cha cha. The strange-sounding Spanish words were sung with wild abandon to a Latin beat. It was with a certain amount of pride that I and my friends mouthed Spanish lyrics, certain only of the correct accent.

One of the happiest moments of my life was when two prose works (which I translated to Spanish) were published in a 1984 issue of *Fem: publicación femenista*, in Mexico City. My father, who had died the year before at age ninety-three, would have been proud.

I write using the best language that I can muster, and listen carefully to how people speak: everyday speech, *caló*, or slang. I try for a level of language that fits the story. In *The Wedding*, most of the characters were school dropouts and spoke the vernacular of a 1950s Califas barrio. It was a challenge to stay at a level of speech that was believable. Prior to writing, I thought of screening old fifties movies, but much of what was out there was Angloese, not Chicanismos.

My forthcoming book, *Hoyt Street: Autobiography*, is said to be quite literate. Much of this is due to my development as a teacher, and the need to express myself within an academic environment. I think it is important to students that an instructor use a level of language that they can learn from and aspire to. I do use jargon and slang, much of it learned from my children.

To me good writing—like good poetry—means good word usage. I dislike everyday language. Rather, I need to hear new words, sounds, inflections that transcend the mundane. A favorite poet is Rosemary Catacalos, who merges Greek mythology with *caló*.

Lyricism in literature is important to me, yet in writing, difficult to achieve. Often, through the use of metaphors, this can be achieved, but not always. Tone is equally important and one that, when teaching, I tend to harp on. If nothing else, my students leave class knowing something of "the emotional tone of a piece." I prefer a good psychological novel to one that merely entertains. Mexican and Latin American writers have a good grasp on lyricism and tone; Anglo-American writers do not.

I have been greatly influenced by the writings of Rosario Castellanos, Nelly Campobello, José Donoso, Elena Garro, Juan Rulfo (a favorite), Ramón Sender, Ana María Matute, Italo Calvino, and, of course, Elena Poniatowska. As a child

I avoided comic books like the plague. Too many pictures and not enough words. Early on I got hooked on the works of Maugham, Steinbeck, Greene. Favorite works were *The Razor's Edge* and *Leave Her to Heaven*. Each summer I headed for the local library, then read from dawn to dusk.

Reading is my passion. I would rather read than write and do not begrudge the hours spent reading. I read ten books at a time. I began with two then moved on to three, and so forth. I cannot stand not to know what is in the other books! So I read them all at the same time. Once I return to a book, the story, characters, and plot immediately return. When I discover an author that I like, I read all of her/his books. A recent discovery is Brian Moore, author of *Blackrobe*. I've read six of his novels (set in Montreal, Europe, and New York).

Reading is important to my writing and to my teaching. While I read tons of academic works, I try to keep up with fiction, especially by Latin American, Mexican, Asian, Black, and Indian writers. I very much like Naguib Mahfouz (*Palace Walk* and *Palace of Desire*), and everything by Bharati Mukherjee.

I read for pleasure and rarely study a book, let alone take notes. Once I am finished with a work I go on to others, aware, however, that writers influenced other writers. I never wanted to be a literary critic, but when I was in New Mexico I reviewed books for the *Albuquerque Journal* and recently for *Belle Lettres*, which could mean I am now a critic. But overall, I read for the adventure, joy, and experience expressed in a written work.

I buy more books than clothes. When in the hospital to give birth to my children, I packed baby booties—and two to three books! Once, when on a camping trip to Baja, I packed eleven books into a pillowcase and upon arrival could not find them. Someone had hidden them as a joke! Undaunted, I walked to the corner Conasupo, a communal market. There I discovered books published by Cuadernos Mexicanos, among them *Hasta no verte Jesús mío*, and works by Rojas-González,

Martín Luis Guzmán, and Jesús Gardea. I bought the entire batch for a small pittance. I once told Elena Poniatowska I discovered her *entre las cebollas.*

Death and dying are recurrent themes in my work. One could say I have a fetish about death. When my brother Rito died I absorbed my parents' pain. I remember everything about his death: the black *carroza* that brought him home for the last time—then took him to Valhalla Cemetery in Burbank, the stench of flowers—gardenias and buttercups pinned to a sheet—the taste of hot chocolate and sweet *pan*. The image of my father and male relatives carrying Rito's coffin to church is etched in my memory, and so is that of my mother walking home as I trailed behind her. I can still feel each rock and pebble along the dirt path.

"The Dress," my first publication, is of a child's search for a dress in which to bury her mother. Death—in the form of tuberculosis—is the theme of "Los Tísicos." It is my favorite work. After writing this work (and aware of the repetition) I was determined not to write again of death or the tubercular, yet this theme reappears in "Enero," written for my mother. Although my father's presence permeates my works, I am my mother's daughter. And as a feminist, I felt obligated to recapture her life, her pain. "Enero" is dedicated to her.

The short story is my forté, but I have written some plays. When in eighth grade at Pacoima Elementary (I was thirteen), I wrote the play staged for our January graduation. It was terribly corny and trite, but I got to select the cast, and for a time I was very popular. I borrowed a table and lamp from our house, all of which my family later recognized. Yet no one told me I was a writer and should develop this talent. In May of that same year I wrote a similar play for Mother's Day dedicated to *las madres.* My mother attended and appeared proud of me. This time I got to play the lead.

In 1990, when at the University of New Mexico, bored to tears during the holiday break, and with nothing new to write, I wrote "Blanca's Wedding," a play based on my novel

The Wedding. I first read books on playwriting and watched numerous plays, both on video and at the university. I then decided that I did not have to be a playwright. Still, "Blanca's Wedding" was almost staged by the theater group at New Mexico State University. Because I was immersed in studies, I could not revise it to their specifications. I hope to finish it soon, then write the screenplay.

Writing is hard work. I will rewrite a story until it is per-fect . . . be it seven or eight times. I revised "Los Tísicos," a favorite piece, at least ten times.

Much of my writing is experimental. I feel the need to move away from the short story. The poet in me is slowly emerging, but I hate lyric verse and have yet to master meter. Just now I am immersed in writing biographies, and I re-cently completed biographies of five Hispanic New Mexican women. Before I try something new, I study the form. I am not an essayist, but I know the form. In time I hope to write a book of personal essays, but not just yet.

Writing is my gift, my obligation. A way to correct nega-tive stereotypes of *mexicanos*, recapture the past, and validate the Chicano experience. I want the world to know of the love and *honor* inherent in Mexican culture, of our *gente's* strug-gle to make a life in a country that disdained and systemati-cally oppressed them. Although I write of California, my experience is both universal and specific. I write for my chil-dren, but also for my siblings. That they may remember.

I never set out to write an autobiography. Rather, I got used to the first person: I. More importantly, I realized the importance of social history and of writing of everyday life. While writing of my life might be interpreted as *hubris*, more and more women today write autobiography. Moreover, the first person narrative is more intense and immediate, and allows the reader to share an intimate experience with the writer.

I write to tell stories. Stories in which the characters have names like López, Gómez, García. Stories that blend humor and irony, but also love. *The Wedding* is a love story, and although the bride and groom were not concerned with the nineties fetish with intimacy, they did love each other.

Finally, I write to give voice to *mujeres: abuelas, tías, hermanas, amigas.* To call forth the ghosts of mexicanas who paved the way for us. Women like Emma Tenayuca, labor organizer during the 1938 San Antonio pecan shellers' strike, repeatedly incarcerated for being a communist. I want to write of the 1931–33 repatriation of *familias mexicanas* to Mexico, of that Sunday in January when they were rounded up inside the Los Angeles *placita*, then put into trains headed south. Hundreds were repatriated to Mexico because of nativism and fear that immigrants were taking jobs away from white Americans. I need to tell of 1930s Gallup, New Mexico, mining strike when Italian, Polish, Mexican, and Irish women, in an effort to stop strikebreakers, bared their breasts—and saved the day.

I am still developing as a writer. My two books were experiments in characterization, plot, and dialogue. *Hoyt Street: Autobiography* is to date my best work but was held up when I changed publishers. I hope to write until I'm ninety. Like Gary Soto, I write for those who cannot. For those who lack words or fear to take pen to paper to give vent to memory and pain.

RITA MAGDALENO

Hermanita

We were old enough. Sí, old enough to go con mi Papá. That
night, the moon was coming up like a mistake, like an eye
punched out, swollen like a calabacita, so soft and puffy. It
was the bluish color of a little plum squeezed too hard. Sí, the
moon was a mistake coming up that night in Grover Canyon
over the tailings of Inspiration Mine and all the stripped hills;
over gray horses in the next canyon and the sad little songs
that José strummed on his guitar; over the jojoba and the Alamo
trees; over the two Holly Berry and our small back porch. It
was winter, November, our back yard ice cold. And you, hermanita, went to sleep forever. Señor, why did you take her? I
got down on my knees and prayed, "Oh, sweet Jesus, you are
so kind. Por favor, Dios, give us your blessings and deliver us
from evil." But my Mama still opened her legs and let the
little death slide again. You, coming wet and red into the
house, into the big brown hands de la Señora Flores. Pobrecita, mi hermanita. I prayed and prayed for you.

That night, after everyone fell asleep, Papá came. "Come
on, wake up . . . Shhh. Carmen y Chayo, levántense. Get up."
And we put on our shoes, wrapped white blankets around our
shoulders como Indias, like little ghosts con ponchos. It was
like a holy ceremony and we were putting on white vest-
ments. We were following our Papá out to the back yard in
Grover Canyon. Hush! Callado . . . calladito, quiet. Shhh!
And I saw the pale bruised moon. She hung above us as we
made our little procession into the night, la Noche Triste.

Hermanita, you never got a name. That night, we wrapped

you in a little silk scarf, slipped you back into the earth, into Grover Canyon, into Nuestra Madre. Our Mother—la Mujer Buena. Buena, Good Mother. Sí, we slipped you into la tierra bendita because there was no money to bury you, pobrecita. It nearly broke my father's heart, his big corazón. He was a good father, hermanita. He took his shovel and cut the ground open, made a little hole in the earth for you. The land in our back yard was so hard, muy duro. Clank, clank . . . cold shovel in my ear.

That winter, I was almost thirteen and my eyes were as black as ripe olives. Hermanita, I wonder what color your eyes would have been. Sí, almost thirteen; almost a woman— I was old enough. Es la verdad. Como mi Papá me dijo a mí y a Carmen, "Don't go to sleep tonight. We're going to bury your little sister. You are old enough to help me." And I was proud pa' ayudar a mi Papá, proud to help him. Sí, I was old enough. That' what he told me. And it's the truth . . . es la verdad.

THE JUNGLE GYM

Marcos de Niza, the jungle gym
and our small tangled lives.
My mother and I are posing
for a photo, black and white
images already weaving into
the cool gray arms of the jungle
gym. My mother's crystal pendant
catches the light of soft yellow
sun, bright as a wish, her dream
to return to the circus,
artistin, she called herself,
acrobat, post-war Europe.

Marcos de Niza, morning glories
and my mother. She is wearing red
lipstick, a rust-brown sweater,
her breasts very full, small gold
pin in her hair and a simple wedding
band on her right hand, European style.
Behind us, the boys are playing
basketball and my mother is holding
me safe, dangling me in front of her,
my legs loose and very free. I straddle
the gray bar as if riding a shiny
stick horse, white cap on my head
and the shadow of my father coming
across me now, weaving its way
through the gray bars.

Marcos de Niza, brown boys
and the morning glories.
They are stretching blue
across our gray housing project,
shadow of my father reaching now
across my white dress,
the jungle gym winding cool
as seaweed all around us–
around me, around my war bride
mother, around the shadow
of my father still washing up
long and dark against me.

THE PENNY GAME

On Sundays
on the east side
of the house on Maricopa
Patsy would call out

"Venga . . . come up
to the tree," everything
quiet and brown
on Sundays

toda la familia
there all afternoon
cooking sopa and warming
tortillas all afternoon

on Sundays and the girls
would go up into the tree
with Patsy all afternoon
and learn the secret place

for the penny
take it and hide it
in a place where no one
could find it except Patsy
moving warm and brown
in small wet circles
girls with red dresses
full of ruffles

"Don't tear your dress,
mijita," our tías would
tell us and it was easy
to breathe in that place.
in the tree

little breaths and wet
fingers looking for the penny
in June and Patsy

wild girl with black hair
gold studs in her warm
ear lobes and red
dress, red ruffles

showing off the penny
game in June and small fingers
warm as leaves in the big tree
trembling green.

MEMORIAL

for Alois Kramer, my grandfather

I
1947, European Spring, season
of reconciliation, reconstruction,
you serving up your war stories
on a table wiped clean for your
toothless friends, smell of cigars
and sweat, three dead sons.
You are waving your hands
across your memories.

2
France, 1964, a crest of white
crosses, half a century of forgotten
dates. The soldiers are sleeping
under soft moss, pale sun crawling

over each green plot and your son,
Fritz. Finally, you are claiming
his small lost grave.

3

Opa, I remember the dead rabbit
you showed me, once. He was a bony
creature, barely enough to feed us.
You cracked his spine and I watched
the blood, the nerves. They traveled
like a pinkish gray dream inside
that fragile white column of bones.

4

During the war, German nuns always
baptized the babies so they wouldn't
go to Limbo. Holy Sacrament
of Baptism, water trickling
over each bloody head.

5

Sometimes, I still sit by the window
while everyone sleeps. I can hear
the wind spinning, red shawl
around my shoulders, holy
wind and water to wash
away so many sins.

6

Old man, now I understand the way
you had to gum your stories,
teeth dropping out one by one,
milk bread in your bowl,
white mush. You kept

the memory of a black boot
inside your jaw, a mouthful
of teeth taking shape
around my neck. It is
the evidence
of my liberation.

SMALL GESTURES

You are sleeping beside me
without memories, candles
and the smell of cinnamon tea
on the stove, silk music,
skin, moonlight running
across my window ledge
in November, month before
my mother's death. You are sleeping
beside me without memories, brief
liver, night smells. Cinnamon
and sweat, the fierce way
I loved you, slowly, your head
nesting in my elbow, breathing,
my mother's breath still warm
like a small bird dark bird in my memory.
This wish, my longing
that would make your hand unfold,
wing brushing my cheek, delicate.

*   *   *

It is always the small gestures
which make us human—mothers
combing their daughters' hair;

washing a child's hands; gathering
red clover and jasmine for sun tea,
leaves heavy and wet. Mother,
the memory of you came today
in a small card, reprint, "In the Garden,"
mother and child, oil on canvas, a gift,
your childhood friend writing to me,
"I remember so well, your mother with you
in her arms as we sent her off, the train
station, 1947, my god, where has time gone?"

* * *

Night is spilling into the window, generous
air, chaparral quivering in the arroyo,
a clump of stars hovering above the house.
At dawn, moonlight will scatter yellow
through brittlebush and my heart
will crawl out of its cove of grief,
your hands moving quietly
through my dark hair.

GRENZE

This damp Saturday morning, our train clicks
steady and slow, east to Berlin. I sit
with three old women, our small brown
compartment heavy with smoke. Two of these
women are from Augsburg and one of them
is my godmother, my German aunt; the other
woman comes from the east, Saalfeld.
They are smoking, drawing deeply on H.B.

cigarettes; they are discussing the reconstruction
of the east, last week Berlin hailed as the new
capitol by a narrow margin of votes.
"We'll have to pay for everything," they mutter
and I watch the land slide green against
my window, an old village cemetery
suddenly standing up in thick wet grass.
Now, we are pulling through Ludwigstadt
and the east German woman is saying,
"Look! We are coming to the border."
She is beginning to tell us about
the long separation from her mother
who lives in the west, Erlangen. She
is explaining how they were split
by the border, *die Grenze*, for more
than forty years. And now we are stopping
in Probstzella, border town where I go
to an open window, lean out and look
for remnants of the old wall. Here,
I can imagine the way of *der Polizei* guarded
this famous line of freedom. Here, I can see
how that sharp division between east and west
has already fallen away. Here, I see a solitary
finch and the old faces of grey houses staring
back at me. Here, I can feel an old separation—
of heart and land, of mother and daughter. This
trip is like going back more than forty years
and I'm thinking of my dead mother, of the borders
we once constructed between one another.
                    But now Germany speaks
            of reunification and all of us—
            mothers and daughters —are traveling

freely from west to east across
die Grenze, wet border. She is
wide open like a mother
who is ready
to give birth.

PAT MORA

IT MAY BE DANGEROUS

No sound. The child watches us
and the lake, flat as an old mirror.

No wind, no ripples or waves
just three of us, until the creature rises.

The child's face is my mother's.
She wears a white dress with puff-sleeves.

Or is it my daughter that gazes at me
still as a photograph from years away?

Even when the head rises from the lake
there are no ripples. I open my palm to it.

Its breath is warm, and I want to stroke
the long muzzle of this moose, perhaps.

But I feel what the man doesn't: the child
watches me. There are teeth in this warm mouth

and the child watches. I am the middle woman,
not my mother, not my daughter.

I am a woman standing on the edge of a lake
holding a mouth in my hand, and there is no sound.

EVEN IN LOS ANGELES

1

In any dark, I feel his little hands slowly rub my
legs, even here, in this apartment,
I keep my curtains closed, and when the owners leave,
I turn on every light, for a *duende* is sly
and could hide in any whispering corner, at the base
of any plant. His hands like old leaves wait for my
bare legs. Even here, I hear his breath whir
when I walk quickly down the silent hall.

2

In Guatemala, he'd ride the moonlight horses outside
our house, grasp their manes and spin them round
the corral as if he were on a merry-go-round gone wild.
"*Oyelo*," my father muttered. "*Oye al duende*."
At dawn he'd disappear. The horses gasped and panted,
rolled their exploding eyes, until my father calmed them,
snipped their manes woven in a braid so tight
only scissors could unweave the work.

3

"Wyooooooo," *el duende* whistled from the *ceiba*
near our house, a mountain of a tree. "Wyoooooooooooo,"
he whistled, whistled to me, the sound in that heat
cool and clear as a cold stream. Days he'd sleep
in the tree's hum. Nights he'd spit on his fingers,
slick his hair, leap about avoiding light. Waiting.
Would my father trade me for a bag of gold?
"Emma," *Duende* called me, "wyooooooooooooooo, Emma."

4

One night, his whistle wrapped around my waist
and pulled me to the tree. My mother shouted
like a howler monkey, but I could only move into his sound.
My legs began to swell, my tongue filled my mouth, then
one step from his fingers, my mother grabbed my braid.
She hit and slapped my face, and head and legs and broke
the spell. For days, I spoke no word, but I could hear
his whistle sweet as honeywine. My father burned the tree.
My mother whispered, "*Nunca*. Never trust the dark."

DOÑA ANA

I can barely see her rocking in the dark. Wind and rain bang
window slats, slash palm trees. We're women caught
in a storm of stories. In the hills rivers are being born. They
    plunge
through bougainvillea into the hiss of the island's green snake
or into *barrios*, oozing with sewage into cardboard houses,
    agua negra.

"I could hear their whimpers from across the street," she says,
her voice worn, like an old, familiar record,
the voice of *tías* and *abuelitas*, the voice of storytellers.
"Every afternoon they kicked and shoved *mis muchachos*
into the police yard, into the sun until the boat and its
    turistas
left. *Lloraban*. I'd hear the children cry and cry, '*Mamá,
    Mamá*,'
and then the beatings would begin. '*¡Por Dios!*' I'd yell. '*Son
    niños*.'

Ay los blanquitos y su dinero. Their soft hands come for
   amber,
and pink mangoes, not to see skinny children, open palms.
Un horno. Los policías baked them in that heat. Right to their
   bones,
pobrecitos. No shade, no water, and so we bought a little
   house
where they could hide. "*Qué tristeza,*" she says shaking
   her head
and rocking. "It's our country, and we have to hide."

Wind runs round and around the widow's home
like children chasing themselves in the rain,
their mouths open, ready to swallow whatever falls from
   the sky.

                                        Dominican Republic

STEPHEN D. GUTIÉRREZ

from *Diary of a Madman*
by Walter C. Ramírez

*Editor's note: My friend Walter Ramírez asked me to include "Diary"
in this collection as a favor to him, since no one else would take it;
he was a colleague of mine at Fresno City College. We both taught
part-time, enjoyed parties and fights on the tube. I got to know him
pretty well. We discovered we had even more in common. We're both
from L.A., slobs, and fundamentally lazy. Walter was smart, with
many wayward opinions, but they were credible. When I told him
yes, that I would publish this piece, he turned ashen and cried on my
shoulder. The next semester he quit teaching on some medical pre-
tense and was seen less and less frequently in public. Finally he
dropped out of sight altogether. He is believed to be somewhere in
Fresno counting his beads: he is a fundamentally religious man. I
know this from experience. We spent many pleasurable hours together discussing sundry subjects, and he always ended by blessing
me like the pope, In the name of the father, the son, the holy spirit.
Amen.*

*I hope he is all right; his wife says he is. But I hear other things.
Rumors. Wild Stories. Innuendoes. I hope he is all right. "Get back in
the race, baby. There's nobody like you; I like your style." All rights
his. All responsibilities mine. Gutiérrez.*

I. Unpublished Letters to the Bee, Etc.[1]

para la gente de Fresno
para cambio
para the helluvit

December 14, 1990

"Letters to the Editor"
The Fresno Bee
1626 E. St.
Fresno, CA 93786

Today I went to a Christmas party for faculty members of the English Department at Fresno City College; I am a substitute teacher there. In the corner of the room, where the party was, three white males sat hunched telling sexist and racist jokes concerning Jews, women, and, in one case, I strongly suspect, Mexicans and/or blacks.

Disgusted, I leaned over and told one, a big burly man sitting close to me, that I hoped if I ever applied for a tenure-position there, none of them would be on the hiring committee. He was oblivious to my plea, to my remark, to my indignation, caught in the har har camaraderie of the last good one. I was a speck to him: a nagging hispanic at his shoulder (I look young and more like a student than a teacher to some, I suspect); and he had more interesting things to talk about—*Did you hear the one about the . . .*

The circle was not broken—three white men hunched forward, leaning together to tell racist and sexist jokes about their students: yes, that's who they were talking about.

Do I trust them?

No.

Do I want my two-and-a-half-year-old son ever taking a course from the likes of them in the future?

No.

---

1. Private rage, private pain: notebooks of madness, healing.

Do I care if they read this and see my name?

No.

Am I afraid of them?

No.

Do I want them serving on any committee that might evaluate any application of mine for a full-tenure (or indeed any) position there?

No no no no no, I say again: No!

I used to be against affirmative action.

Now I am quickly changing my tune.

Tis the season to be jolly!

Walter C. Ramírez

P.S. Assignment #1, three unnamed professors (I don't know their names): *Jokes and Their Relation to the Unconscious*, by Sigmund Freud. . . . Report to me if you understand it; resign if you don't. . . . Dismissed. . . .

* * *

I sat down at my desk and wrote my letter, furious. It was in my office at Fresno City College, with the dusk coming on and the party hopping in the building next door. I could see them through the plate-glass window having a merry ol' time as I sealed the envelope and stomped to the mailbox on campus.

It was cold in the winter in Fresno. In the lighted building at Fresno State the Creative Writing Staff decided my fate by tossing aside my dossier onto a pile marked UNACCEPTABLE *with a 3 x 5 card taped to the head of the wire basket holding the rejects.*

I was a reject again.[2]

It was cold in the winter in Fresno, and the Creative Writing

2. See my essay, "*lost in ithaca . . . memories from an m.f.a. reject,*" forthcoming (or published by now) in *Buk Hates the Workers, Too: New Underground Writers in America Speak*. Not available in most bookstores, you'll probably get shot looking for it in the university bookstores, but, what the fuck, find it. It's good. I've seen the galleys. I'm in it.

Staff, good eggs all, good men and women (four men one woman involved in the process)[3] *warmed their hands in the small fire blazing from their self-righteousness and pomposity in the office of Peter Godoy,*[4] *head poet.*

Ah, catty comment, they're no better, no worse, than most, but, I should've known better: my stuff gets pretty silly stupid sometimes, and there's no place for it in the academic-literary world of today.

I should've known better.

But I didn't.

I had been hearing BIG TALK among the younger faculty ALL YEAR that they were looking for a CHICANO writer, ideally; they'd *loove* to have one, if they could find one. Uh-huh. *Ain't I Chicano enough? Huh? Huh? Huh? Ain't I the right kind of Chicano? Huh? Huh? Huh?* Wow. Godoy stomped on me in passing, and the archangel Scarton came up behind him with a stick, "Kill him! He's still moving! He's dangerous! He don't have my *standard literary practices. . . ." Help me, friend, I just want to say a few things, and then I'll be gone, presently:*

---

3. WHITE, this was Creative Writing, a *special* search, no other members of the Department, representing other groups—f'rinstance a Chicano on the faculty invited to participate in EVERYTHING ELSE—need apply: they didn't know how to read: only *writers* knew how to read. Uh-huh. Harumph. Harumph. Harumph.

4. Famous working-class poet at Fresno State, who's pretty good, sometimes; pretty bad other times. Mostly just a fair writer like all of us, up and down, but with an exaggerated reputation. A vicious bastard, too, he'll probably come after me after this: Fuck it. I ain't got nothing to lose.

He saw to that himself all right. He gave the thumbs down to my dossier in that session (I heard through the grapevine, reliably enough), which took place, ironically enough, on the same day I was sitting in my English Department party at Fresno City College listening to those idiots next to me.

Did I trust them more at Fresno State?

Fuck no.

I just didn't.

They were all into fame, fortune, the best writing available, *according to their standards*, which were conservative, indeed; look at their writings.

I don't give a fuck about literature lately . . . thwack! thwack!
thwack! . . . I just want to get a few things off my chest as well
as I can without regard to . . . thwack! thwack! thwack! . . .
literary decorum or tradition and then I'll be . . . thwack!
thwack! thwack! . . .

ALL RIGHT ALREADY MAN! I GET THE HINT! I'M NOT YOUR TYPE!
THWACK! THWACK! THWACK!
I DON'T EVEN LIKE M.F.A. PROGRAMS.
"KILL HIM!"
THWACK! THWACK! THWACK!
LORD HAVE MERCY, HERE HE COMES.
"LET'S FINISH HIM, SCARTON. HE'S NOT GOOD. HE'S JUST NOT
*   GOOD."*
AHHHHHHHHHHHH!

Grandmaster[5] of the three ring showed up there; and drank
eggnog from small crystal and handblown tumblers that were
in contrast to their rugged and tarnished working-class hands,
but what the hell, a man had to do what a man had to do
sometimes, and sometimes that involved class, even if you
didn't like it, culture and refinement.

I rushed home and got loaded that night listening to *Elvis'*
Christmas Album sitting in my favorite chair. It was good to
be home again, in the safety of my room with all my books
and shit around me; it was a good album. I put my feet on
the hassock and . . . Damn good album. Sipping my wine . . .

---

5. He's an all right guy, actually, but he hurt me by giving me the *thumbs
down* on my dossier, so I'm just telling the truth of what I think of him: I
never liked his work that much. It had kind of a whiny quality, sometimes;
a hard-edged and brilliant quality, other times.
   And that bugged me. And distracted me. Beyond belief. That occasional
(frequent enough, too frequent) whining, pulling that even crept into the
work of his best students sometimes . . .

Si-lent Night, Ho-ly Night,
All is Calm, All is Bright,
Round Yon Virgin, Mother and Child,
Holy Infant, So Tender and Mild,
Sle-ep in Heavenly Peace, Sle-ep in Heavenly Peace

Si-lent Night, Ho-ly Night . . .

   Song fades to a lovely scene of Fresno; voice speaks over a
birds-eye view of our fair city, adrift in snow and love.
   Morning after morning I scanned the paper for my letter, but
finally gave up. Life would go on chugging as it had in Fresno
for the last five thousand years. I taught my course at City College, Creative Writing, because my friend the poet, Arturo
Peña, was out with cancer, battling the big C through chemo-
therapy, will and guts.
   My friend Arturo Peña, who had been hired against the
wishes of the English Department at Fresno City College by a
fiery Dean, through affirmative action. . . .
   He came over to my house one morning with the poet Aman
Jimínez with a proposition, he said, for me.
   "What is it?" I countered.
   "Teach my class for me, creative writing." He looked me
straight in the eye as he lowered himself into my armchair and
asked Aman for help in Spanish. "I want you." What a beautiful man he was in Spanish, a whole other Arturo I had never
suspected was there: fluid, graceful, more at ease in the world.
I had always found him a little stiff, frankly, plus there was un-
derlying tension between us having to do with Chicano and
Mexican: he was quintessentially Mexican, I am quintessentially Chicano, both of us having, I believe, the best and worst
characteristics of our race (well at least I have the worst characteristics of my race, that's for sure, I . . .): he took too much
in his life, but he was a lovely, lovely man to be around as I got
to know him and he got to know me better and we came to

*trust each other and realize we genuinely respected each other
for some qualities in each other that we gave each other.*

We came to like each other, finally.

*Aman burped and lit a cigarette and darted outside. I told
him he could smoke a cigarette and do anything he wanted in
my house. I liked him a lot. He was a helluva poet, too, one of
the best in Fresno . . .*

*"It's creative writing, fiction, just fiction . . ." Arturo went on
as he waved some smoke away as Aman turned aside, and I got
up and turned on a fan and opened a window.*

Aman got the hint and stood outside . . .

*"Will do, I'll teach your course." I put aside all plans and de-
cided to go for it. I wasn't doing anything, anyway, except the
usual—scanning the want ads for the* IDEAL *job and writing a
few stories while my wife supported me and I took care of the
kid, mostly. I'm a lazy asshole. I'm the first to admit that.
"What do I do?"*

*"Go see the Dean, Wimblaugh, he already has your name.
He's waiting for you."*

*"Okay." Before he left my house I touched his arm. "Thanks a
lot, Arturo, I appreciate it."*

He smiled the way he could, "Anytime . . ."

*Then a few months later he signed his book to me at the
fancy mall in Fresno: "For Walt, Janet and Len. Hope you like
these poems. Thank you for teaching my class. Fresno needs
you. Love, Arturo." And touched me deeply. Who suspected
Arturo of being so political, of caring who exactly taught our
students as long as they were good writers, universal-standard
bearers, arbiters of talent based on objective . . . blah blah
blah . . . blah-blah blah-blah blah-blah . . . Nobody, man.
Everybody thought courteous old Arturo Peña was one of the
boys, a neat liberal; nobody knows what rage seethes beneath
us all, these brown masks, in Fresno and elsewhere . . .*

*So he signed his book to me at Fig Garden Bookstore, amidst
the rich and famous, writers of the time. I turned away and*

went home. Later that year I applied for a job as Creative Writing Professor at California State University, Fresno.

I didn't get the job. Below are more excerpts from my journal chronicling my dejection over this incident and others: madness, pain, rage, par for the course . . .

I'm still teaching my course at City College, by the way, until the Dean tells me otherwise . . . She's a beautiful black woman who understands me, I think, smiled at me in a certain way (or am I misunderstanding it: the brotherhood/sisterhood of . . . what? bemused outsiders? . . . wow . . . something special about that woman, anyway, a detached quality from it all . . . and a wonderful warm smile that sets my heart a-spinning); and who might cut me some slack: not make me a regular tenure-track teacher to teach this peach of a course, but let my brown ass hang around as long as I do a decent job with our students.

For reasons of her own. Of our own.

She's a new hire, and what does that say about attitudes in the English Department, and Administration at Fresno City College and elsewhere in the valley? Not much. I still think that there are great walls, great barriers of white arrogance and resistance, to smash through . . .

I don't want a tenure-track job at City College, by the way; too much teaching, frankly. I applied for the one at Fresno State because it was less teaching and it seemed like the right thing to do—big time and all that shit, plus I wanted to work with students/writers from their freshman year to graduation or perpetual enrollment in the big college of life.

I liked the prospect of that.

But noooooooooo—the powers that be wouldn't have it. I wasn't good enough, frankly, to rate even an interview.

So below continues my short chronicle of these depressing days following the letdown, *that* blow, *footnoted recently to make more sense, for those of you not familiar with the Fresno literary scene.*

For those of you not familiar with the Fresno literary scene at all, you might want to skip this piece and go on to the next one.[6] It's pretty literary here.

For those of you beat, underground writers out there, I think you'll know what I mean. This one's for you, too, and all the gente in Fresno alienated and outcast, and all the . . . Everybody and everything, man, this one's for you . . .

> *Yours, Paz,*
> *Ramirez*
> *March, 1991*

* * *

Then sometime in there there was a search for the President at FSU. Everybody was excited at the prospect of having a new WHITE president who would be open to the hispanic, sensitive to minority aspirations and issues besetting the community.

I'm beginning to write like the Bee.

It was cold in the winter in Fresno, but now spring was coming on and the Creative Writing Staff had chosen a woman,[7] ranked high on the list of final candidates, to fill the Creative Writing position I had applied for: me, a mere Cornell graduate,[8] 5 publications, 4 of them major publications, but 2 of them are hispanic *let's be serious, one funky magazine with my crazy beat story of L.A. and a groovy drawing by an artist to go with it, stellar recommendations and, most important, rapport with these students at FSU: I was looking forward to working with them, or being given a chance to say why I thought I would be good for them.*

---

6. The author was contemplating a volume of his own, *Oscar Acosta Walked This Way: Notes from a Chicano Underground*. He never got around to it, demoralized as he was by the subsequent events detailed in this piece. I hope he gets back to it. *Editor's note*.

7. I wish her well; from the bottom of my heart, I do . . .

8. God I'm sounding snotty; I'm not concerned with that shit, frankly: sorry.

*I had mentioned in my cover letter that I had worked success-
fully with one, a Chicano,[9] who had gotten a story accepted in
a national magazine, The Bilingual Review, but hispanic; other
students had touched me by their sympathy for my application.
Homeboys from CWAA—Chicano Writers & Artists Association—
who I barely knew came up to me on campus that fall semester
while I was substituting for a sick teacher there, and shook my
hand, "I heard you're applying, man. That's great. We need
somebody, man. We need a Chicano. These people flip out if
you throw a Spanish word on them; only Godoy . . ."[10]*

*I was touched. I had never known the full extent of Chicano
alienation on this campus; homeboys from the small towns just*

9. I didn't mention that. I knew that would have gotten my ass kicked out
immediately. A semester before, a friend of mine—the Chicano member of
the faculty—had gotten into it with an old professor who had referred a Chicano candidate for a literature position to the Chicano Studies Department
because the applicant had had the audacity to mention in his letter that, in
addition to his regular English courses, he would like to help minority students on campus in any way he could.

I knew one had to stay de-ethnic in these matters, universal-sterile and
safe; until you got in . . .

10. To give him his due: he's been wonderful with his students; only not
with this writer: Ha ha ha ha ha.

Here's the punchline, prematurely, for those of you who are antsy readers
waiting for an ending: I must be the only writer in Fresno who Peter Godoy
has not helped.

Ha ha ha ha ha.

Get it? I'm the only one who he has not encouraged.

Ha ha ha ha ha.

In any way.

Anyway, these students would mention a few other teachers/writers who
they thought were good, real good, but then they would mention a few others that they thought were worthless, worth shit.

"Go for it, man, so go for it."

And I would smile and say, "Orale, it's a long haul . . . I don't think I'm
going to get an interview even," half-kiddingly, because I thought I was going
to get an interview, at least.

Ha ha ha ha ha.

Do you get it, man, do you get it? Ha ha ha ha ha. It's *killing* me . . .

don't feel good about their professors, about expressing themselves in their own language, caló,[11] *sharing their own experiences in a group full of white students dominated by* WHITE *thought.*

"What's with all of this Chicano stuff," a graduate student had told a friend of mine in the graduate-level creative writing seminar. "I love this story except for this Chicano stuff."

The teacher didn't see anything wrong. He offered no objection to the student's critical assessment.[12]

IT GOT IN THE WAY, THIS CHICANO STUFF.

But I'm skipping too far ahead now, and will backtrack and try to cover some very basic ground: I had applied for a job at FSU *in the fall of 1990, for a position in* Creative Writing—*the vaunted status of the position didn't impress me: I just wanted to teach the damn kids. I liked them.*[13]

Which brings me to my second point, punto: *I knew some of the Chicano kids, students from helping them along with their writings on the side; my wife was a professor there and preferred some of them to me.*[14]

It worked out well, as I said. I was hoping for a fucking interview *at least, to strut my stuff, blow up my campaign, show them my brilliance and excellence (they thought my writing wasn't excellent: maybe it wasn't.* Big Deal, *the point was,* Who's gonna teach our students? Big point), *so, I would sit there in an interview and wow them with my overall* bril-

11. Chicano slang.

12. I had read the story and thought the Chicano stuff was germane, absolutely crucial to the story: it was what the story was about. Alienation. Hatred. Pain. *Chicano stuff.*

13. All of them, the kids in the valley . . .

14. That's where I get a lot of this inside information from, too, obviously; we've been here five years, since 1986, when we moved 'cross country from Ithaca, NY, where we were both graduate students at Cornell University; me a failure in the M.F.A. program there (see my essay, *"lost in ithaca . . ."*), her a brilliant but lazy doctoral student in English and American literature. I'm originally from L.A.; she's originally from New Jersey.

liance—I'm very smart, actually, and smarter than 95% of the faculty I was applying to, I would say, and that's the IRONIC *part of it all*[15]*—and confidence and competence*[16] *and excellence—actually, my writing wasn't that bad, either; it's pretty good, has some strengths and virtues that even* PETER GODOY'*s writing doesn't, has some weaknesses too shared by none of the staff; but it's vice-versa there, par for the course.*[17]

I was as good as, in some respects, as qualified as, in all respects, all the younger members of the Creative Writing there at Fresno State.

But noooo, not even a fucking interview.

I remembered my friend Richard the trusty: "What? They're hiring Chicanos at Fresno State? Ah ha ha ha . . . That's a good one, ese, that's a good one; who's ever telling you that's got

---

15. God I feel embarrassed saying this. I feel so fucking *dumb*, too.

16. I'm a competent minority! I'm a competent minority! Teacher, teacher, can you see my hand waving?!

"He's nuts."

"He's not for us. He likes CHARLES BUKOWSKI even."

KING OF THE UNDERGROUND, KING OF THE FACTORIES, FINALLY.

"HELP ME BUKOWSKI!"

"FUCK YOU! YOU'RE GETTING TOO CLOSE, KID. I GOT MY LITTLE PATCH IN THE GARDEN, TOO. HAVE A CIGAR, GODOY?"

"I ALWAYS KNEW WE'D LIKE EACH OTHER ONCE WE MET; WE'RE TWO OF THE SAME KIND."

"GRRRRRRRRR."

SUCCESS SUCCESS SUCCESS I want my drink of water too, and will do anything for it, bend over backwards, apply for grants, meet the right people, get invited—slimy practice—to submit to magazines—go to conferences, MEET THE RIGHT PEOPLE, AGAIN, shake hands and smile, get in their magazines high gloss reprints when will it end?

Whatever happened to the old editor-writer relationship, hardcore writers doing it on their own with no boon except for their talents?

It was probably never that way.

I'm the last of the hardcore writers.

I just want to impress an editor without him knowing anything about me . . .

17. I do the working-class thing as well as Him, sometimes; sometimes better: you could look it up.

some gripe up his sleeve he can't handle. Affirmative action, shit."

He swept up the floor, the space allotted to him to take care of.

It was on the second floor of the Fresno County Jail where I was in the drunk tank for fucking up, and I knew him from boxing when I used to work out at the Southeast Fresno boxing Club.[18] *"Doing Mexicans favors . . . ah ha ha ha. You asshole, man; when's your old lady gonna pick you up. You're beginning to stink."*

I rattled the bars of the cage. I still am, rattling the bars of the cage, wherever I go . . .

It went down like this finally:[19] *the woman they chose was the first on the list of final candidates.* SHE WAS THE ONLY ONE, *finally, because the #2 was a* CUBAN *who though prolific, was deemed at the last minute insufficient to fill those shoes of* CREATIVE WRITING *Professor at Fresno State.*

Fishy, Fishy, eh?

How did he get so high on the list finally if he was so bad? Seems like to me as soon as the real possibility of hiring a his-

---

18. I ran into a parked car with my bicycle and proclaimed Dostoevsky to the owner, who came out of the bar shouting, "Hey, that's my new car!"

"Love, love is the answer. . . .

"Call the cops and get that asshole out of here; he's dangerous. He looks dangerous. . . ."

"No, I'm not dangerous . . ."

By the time the cops came I was three doors down still trying to make my getaway, "No, ocifer, let me explain . . ."

"Sure, come here . . ."

Clink. Bench. Bars.

"Hey, Richard . . ."

"Hey Walt, you crazy motherfucker, what're you doing here?"

"Trying to spread the word; nobody'll listen."

"Yeah?"

"Yeah."

"Shit."

19. What follows below is all hearsay, but it's hearsay that I believe; my wife couldn't attend the final hiring meetings because I had applied for the job. But it's hearsay that I believe.

panic, a non-white conventional writer[20] *came around, the deck was reshuffled pretty fast.*

If I've said any lies here, if I've hurt anybody's feelings . . . fuck it . . . feelings are not to be taken into account in this business: and that's a fact.

You could look it up.

Anyway, like to thank all the Chicano students for giving me support; like to thank the black secretary of the English Dept. at Fresno State for giving me the black power salute when I walked into the office one day to pick up some papers for my wife. You beautiful, beautiful woman, Daisy Mason, you . . . choked me up that day, man, you really did.[21]

So there was an FSU presidential search at the time. The search was tarnished. There was no hispanic on the search committee to lend credence to our concerns. When it was over, the search, of course there was no hispanic on the finalists' list: do you really think whites are gonna go out of their way to hire a hispanic when they're not being pushed by hispanics or crazy mad whites to do so?

---

20. Any apologies to the woman they just hired . . . I don't know what kind of stuff she's writing . . . I hope she's good . . . I hope she's righteous . . . that are due: I humbly offer.

You're dealing with a madman, baby. Sock 'em and pop 'em. Go to the head go to the body. I mean go to the body go to the head. *Strut your stuff and don't let* anybody *fuck with you.* Body head. Head body. NO WONDER I GOT MY ASS KICKED AT THE SOUTHEAST FRESNO BOXING CLUB. No, I did all right there, sometimes: 'nother essay.

"Sloppy! He's bothering me!" Scarton trampling across the leaves as I slither away, "Git him! Git him! Git his fucking ass! We cain't have this! I want control!" Butthole tight control.

So does Godoy, for that matter, in his poems.

Loosen up, boys! It's only a game.

21. She's up against it, too. The Department Chair has been after her BLACK ass all year, to fire her; she overheard him saying he was going to use his "Stepin Fetchit routine" to get some thing from somebody, once, and was mortified, offended, disturbed . . . called him on it and got her ass hanged, in hot water, ever since . . .

He's a weasel of a man, sly and slimy, who I expect to be appointed Dean any day now . . .

Of course not.

So there was a little brouhaha, a minor temblor, finally.

Hispanic groups objected to the search process.

Flim flam shim sham on the part of the University brought a few token hispanics to oversee the final stages of the job search: the interviews and all that shit . . .

. . . some of the hispanics had the balls and good sense to call it like they saw it, like it was: tokenism . . .

. . . other hispanic groups wanted to halt the whole process . . .

That's where we come in again (this is getting boring, isn't it? this part of the narrative? Fuck Art, I'm not trying to create literature or write well here, only communicate and save my soul, my ragged jagged edge of a tin can soul—shantih shantih shantih—peace).

The Bee wrote a silly condemnatory editorial dismissing hispanic concerns basically and saying BUSINESS AS USUAL, again.

A home boy I knew fired off a letter denouncing the Bee's flim flamism and hypocrisy.[22]

Peter Godoy is a good man[23] but is an old man and must go.[24]

The new writer, Walter Ramirez, robed in saffron, steps forward on the long parapet that is Fresno, the Fresno literary scene—shantih shantih shantih—

I used to like this fucking town. I used to love this fucking town.

---

22. Omitted here because he tried to fuck me recently in a POWER move at the college. Ha ha, you blew it: your chance to be famous.

(Actually it's better than mine, and that's why it's omitted.)

I got fired up and wrote one myself (I reprint the whole damn thing for your benefit)—shantih shantih shantih—Eliot turns in his grave and is a Royalist and all that shit.

23. And I'm not even sure of that, either. O mystery of life . . . shantih shantih shantih . . .

24. And I'm not sure of that, either. O this painful, painful project . . . ejected from paradise. . . .

I used to believe I belonged in this town; now, no more . . . shantih . . . up your ass . . . with a . . . GODOY . . . I'M THE BEST WRITER IN TOWN . . . And I know that's not true, either. But to be treated like dirt, like shit . . . shantih shantih shantih . . . not even a fucking interview . . . and to be condescended to by these pricks in CREATIVE WRITING . . . mediocre writers, average writers all of them . . . with strengths and weaknesses, too . . . "we're looking for a Chicano writer, this year" . . . shantih . . . ly lace . . . it's absurd . . . the pomposity of the white race, of people in power . . . shantih shantih shantih . . .

I hope to pick up tomorrow and make more sense, peace to all, and I mean that. Shantih shantih shantih.[25]

Whoever said that is a shit, whether it was the Department Chair—Bayard Sart—or the young Southern writer—SCAR-TON—who did as much as anybody to keep me out of Fresno State, from getting an interview—"too disjunctive" I heard he commented about my narrative to another colleague in dismissing my application. Well fuck me in the ass I'll write STRAIGHT narrative from here on in—WHOEVER SAID THAT COMMENT IS A SLIMEBALL PIECE OF SHIT, WHETHER IT WAS THE DEPARTMENT OR YOU, BOYD SCARTON, IN ONE OF YOUR MOMENTS OF CHICKENSHIT SELF-REVELATION OF WHO YOU REALLY ARE—A RUTHLESS CHICKENSHIT BASTARD SON OF A BITCH; whoever said that, whoever is responsible for that comment, and I have a feeling it's not the Department Chair, but Scarton's own nefarious chickenshit way of trying to get back at this Chair who he had a beef with, is a chickenshit son of a bitch slimeball piece of shit WHO SHOULD NOT BE TEACHING AT FRESNO STATE ANY MORE THAN THE HEAD OF THE KU KLUX KLAN SHOULD BE TEACHING AT MOOREHOUSE STATE UNIVERSITY.

25. Special apology to the Department Chair, who might not be a shit. What I was really thinking of, was this: a friend of mine—Chicano, professor—got told by a colleague of his—white, Southern—SCARTON—that the Department Chair was having a hard time getting rid of Daisy Mason, but in the meantime he had gotten rid of three or four brown faces—student workers—around him in the English Department office.

Straight enough, Scarton?

Straight enough, gentlemen?

Settle it between you and put an apology in the mailbox of every brown face who ever worked in the English Department during your tenure there. Peace, Ramírez.

Shantih shantih shantih. I'm going nuts. I can't go on, I must go on. I can't go on writing without the approval of big PAPA GODOY. Out, Godoy, out. You must.

This must get published.

Life must go on.

I must not let anything impede my talent.

Shantih. *Our father—Who art in heaven—Bow down with me, O reader, and pray this message of balm and healing— Hallowed be thy name—Thy kingdom come—Thy will be done—On earth—as it is in heaven—Give us this day—Our daily bread—And forgive us our trespasses—As we forgive those—Who trespass against us—And lead us—Not into temptation—But deliver us from evil—Amen.*

Greatest poem ever written, and I'll stand by that one, yes I will.

Shantih shantih shantih.

* * *

February 19, 1991

"Letters to the Editor"
The Fresno Bee
1626 E. St.
Fresno, CA 93786

Last December I sent you a letter concerning discriminatory attitudes at Fresno City College. You did not publish it. In the wake of recent controversy surrounding the FSU presidential search I have decided to resubmit it. If you publish it, fine. It is the least you could do towards honoring your pledge to air hispanic concerns about hiring in this valley.[26] If you don't, my gravest suspicions are simply reconfirmed: you are part of the problem, a liberal institution so pompous and arrogant in its assumptions of fairness and impartiality towards minorities in this valley that it boggles the imagination.

So below is a letter (dated December 14, 1990, italicized): I believe it is fare for a family entertainment newspaper and can see no other reason for your reluctance to publish it other than good old-fashioned bigotry and/or cowardice.

Perhaps I should elaborate: your initial refusal to publish it smacks of complicity in the mind-set that permeates this valley: yahoo-ism at every level of culture and society in this valley.

December 14, 1990

Today I went to a Christmas party for faculty members of the English Department at Fresno City College; I am a substitute teacher there. In the corner of the room, where the party was, three white males sat hunched telling sexist and racist jokes concerning Jews, women, and, in one case, I strongly suspect, Mexicans and/or blacks.

Disgusted, I leaned over and told one, a big burly man sitting close to me, that I hoped if I ever applied for a tenure-position there none of them would be on the hiring committee. He was oblivious to my plea, to my remark, to my indignation, caught in the har har camaraderie of the last good one. I was a speck to him: a nagging hispanic at his shoulder (I look young and more like a student than a teacher to some, I suspect); and he had more interesting things to talk about—Did you hear the one about the . . .

The circle was not broken, three white men hunched for-

---

26. I misremembered the editorial in the Bee; they made no such pledge. It was simply wishful thinking on my part.

ward, *leaning together to tell racist and sexist jokes about their*
students: yes, that's who they were talking about.

Do I trust them?

No.

Do I want my two-and-a-half-year-old son ever taking a
course from the likes of them in the future?

No.

Do I care if they read this and see my name?

No.

Am I afraid of them?

No.

Do I want them serving on any committee that might evalu-
ate any application of mine for a full-tenure (or indeed any)
position there?

No no no no no, I say again: NO!

I used to be against affirmative action.

Now I am quickly changing my tune.

Tis the season to be jolly.

Walter C. Ramírez

P.S. Assignment #1, three unnamed professors (I don't know
their names): Jokes and Their Relation to the Unconscious, by
Sigmund Freud . . . Report to me if you understand it; resign if
you don't . . . Dismissed . . .

So I confronted the man again, in his office; so he is a
"powerful figure" in the Department, as they say. So it went
like this:

Oh, what the hell. He is a tedious ass. Why relate another
story of another bigoted and perfectly "liberal" leader in our
community?

Stop the presidential search, in the "interest of fairness of
all those concerned." We have not been served fairly.

This is one angry Chicano in this valley getting angrier
at the excuses rendered as to why so and so . . . such and

such . . . there was no hispanic representation on this or that
search for this or that position.

I remain against affirmative action, by the way. I cannot
support a system that potentially discriminates against anybody. But I know, also, that common sense does not, will not,
will never work in this valley or anywhere else to rectify past
wrongs or, more importantly, redress current imbalances in
representation at the top levels of society.[27]

Qualified minority candidates (and there are far, far more
than the powers that be are willing to admit) will still be
overlooked for positions of power in this valley because white

27. I used to think that was a bad sentence. Now I've changed my mind.
You make the call.

I even had a footnote made for it to COVER MY ASS: "God what a bad sentence that was. I began to worry about my sanity there and wonder if it
would be good or bad if I ever got in the Bee."

"Everything is in flux," Heraclitus.

Even you, reader, are dying right now as you read . . .

Let's all love each other . . .

I'm going sappy . . .

My editor's gonna kill me.

Gutiérrez, where are you?

You big-nosed son-of-a-bitch?

Fresno, Modesto Stockton . . .

When I used to go to Chico State I used to take the bus home through the
valley . . . Fresno, Modesto Stockton . . . All the way down to L.A. I would
sit in the back seat of the 'dog hearing those valley names ring out . . .
Fresno, Modesto Stockton . . .

Who knew that I would be so intimately linked with this town . . .

Its savior . . .

Fresno, Modesto Stockton . . . I love you . . .

Godoy . . . I love you . . . Bales . . . I love you . . . Scarton . . . I love
you . . . Checklehans . . . I love you . . .

Fresno, Modesto Stockton . . .

Windshield wipers arcing in the front across the big windshield; stoned, I
sit in the back on my way home . . .

Fresno, Modesto Stockton . . .

I hold a knife blade to the driver's throat and demand off . . .

I'll take over from here, from now on, with all my love . . .

Fresno, Modesto Stockton . . .

liberal institutions like yours still do not consider it a pressing problem that we do not have input into every phase and aspect of this valley. That is evident from the self-serving and smug tone of your editorial supporting the tarnished job search-process for the president at FSU.

It looks bleak in this valley.

But the least we can have is a dialogue between the interested parties who still believe there's some hope in this valley for decency and justice,[28] and not a shutting down of any aberrant voice[29] that calls it like it sees it.[30]

28. Big word! I can use it! Whose are the words, finally, mine or yours? Up for grabs, finally, or what?

Fresno, Modesto Stockton . . .

Her name was Helen and . . . Fresno, Modesto Stockton . . . I launched a thousand ships for her . . . Fresno, Modesto Stockton . . . I loved her so dearly . . . you know who you are, Helen, I fuck you every Saturday at eight o'clock behind the bowling alley . . . Fresno, Modesto Stockton . . .

"What's going on here?"

"Nothing."

Thought police in gray uniforms with a dash of blue on the collars to let us know they're liberal, cool, hip . . . grab my mss. and proclaim, "disjunctive!" blow their whistles and a million minions, minnows? come swimming out of their air to tickle me to death. Ohhh-hoo-hoo . . . lkjnpvijprjm pmopkrpiko ;k,op5i3o-uy1−ojm pk- uj,pi -k1−

29. Not me, whipped and blind I sit in the corner.

Fresno, Modesto Stockton . . .

Still the noises of the city rise up around me . . .

And I loved her . . . eight days a week . . .

Fresno, Modesto Stockton . . .

30. See no evil, speak no evil . . .

Fresno, Modesto Stockton . . . I love you, enough so to . . . eat a donut at your Winchell's half past eight with all the cons milling around, Harleys parked outside, lowriders cruising Blackstone . . . so much pain, in this town . . . *never saw a woman, so alone, so alone* . . . Her name was Fresno, Modesto Stockton . . . Her donuts weren't romantic at all; they tasted rancid with pain and hurt. Still I dipped them into the coffee and thought, "Fresno, Modesto Stockton . . ."

"All Aboard!"

The bus comes round and round . . .

"Who's driving the bus?"

In this valley . . .[31]

Jesus Christ
Walter C. Ramírez
aka
Jesus Christ

What the fuck's going on here? Why didn't somebody publish my letter? Why didn't somebody give me a fucking interview if they're so concerned about their minority students
and such cool liberal writers all wanting to help each other
out and help others, the disenfranchised, the lost, the voice-
less, FIND THEIR VOICE?

WHY DIDN'T SOMEBODY GIVE ME A FUCKING VOICE, FOR JUST
5 MINUTES, AND LET ME PLEAD MY CASE? WHY? WHY? WHY?

"STANDARDS."

FUCK YOUR STANDARDS.

YOU'RE ALL NOT THAT GOOD, YOU'RE ALL NOT THAT BAD. I
DON'T SEE ANY NOBEL PRIZE WINNERS IN THIS YEAR'S CROP.

CROP? DID I SAY CROP?

FRESNO, MODESTO STOCKTON . . .

I am a weed blowing in the wind, unwanted, self-pitying,
sad . . . I'm not self-pitying at all . . . Where's the bus? I'm get-
ting the fuck out of here, but not before I blow this little kiss to
you, Fresno, this little love letter to you . . . Take that and shove
it, Fresno, I love you . . . Fresno, Modesto Stockton . . .

"All aboard!"

"No!" Godoy is still at the wheel . . .

Godoy turns around with a big smile . . .
"Let's give it a whirl then, anyway, around the world . . ."
Godoy, horrified, gets up to leave . . .
So am I, disgusted, in need of love, help . . .
Fresno, Modesto Stockton . . .
31. "There will be peace, in the valley, for me," Elvis . . .

*"Sit in the back and do the working-class strut and I'll write a
poem about it."*

"Where's my fucking voice?"

Fresno, Modesto Stockton . . .

*Exhaust fumes cover me at the curb, bus leaves me
behind . . .*

Fresno, Modesto Stockton . . .

I look around and wonder . . .

*Your wide blue sky hides such pollutants as boggles the mind
and makes me write like the Bee again and basta, man, basta,
I'm going home, wherever that is . . .*

Fresno, Modesto Stockton . . .

*Last part of the letter without any bullshit for those of you
uptight, anal-retentive readers who can't figure it out on your
own. I number myself among you so don't feel bad. I'm the
most neurotic guy in Fresno, but not, motherfuckers, not, psy-
chotic. Got that?*

Fresno, Modesto Stockton . . .

So here is my bitching letter, part III:

So I confronted the man again, in his office; so he is a
"powerful figure" in the Department, as they say. So it went
like this:

Oh, what the hell. He is a tedious ass. Why relate another
story of another bigoted and perfectly "liberal" leader in our
community?

Stop the presidential search, in the "interest of fairness of
all those concerned." We have not been served fairly.

This is one angry Chicano in this valley getting angrier at
the excuses rendered as to why so and so . . . such and
such . . . there was no hispanic representation on this or that
search for this or that position.

I remain against affirmative action, by the way. I cannot
support a system that potentially discriminates against any-

body. But I know, also, that common sense does not, will not, will never work in this valley or anywhere else to rectify past wrongs or, more importantly, redress current imbalances in representation at the top levels of society.

Qualified minority candidates (and there are far, far more than the powers that be are willing to admit) will still be overlooked for positions of power in this valley because white liberal institutions like yours still do not consider it a pressing problem that we do not have input into every phase and aspect of this valley. That is evident from the self-serving and smug tone of your editorial supporting the tarnished job search-process for the president at FSU.

It looks bleak in this valley.

But the least we can have is a dialogue between interested parties who still believe there's some hope in this valley for decency and justice, and not a shutting down of any aberrant voice that calls it like it sees it.

In this valley . . .

Walter C. Ramírez

*   *   *

So I began to write like the Bee, in order to get into the Bee, and failed at that, too, udderly . . .

Squirt squirt squirt me with milk . . . I'm lost in the desert; no . . . Milk milk milk . . . Dripping from somewhere, in Fresno, a cow . . . MOOOO-VE OVER, ROVER,

Get ready for Walt.

Songtime:
Peace Peace Peace
Holy Holy Holy
The Bee The Bee The Bee
is ridiculous
as this letter,
& you, reader, white liberal,

when it comes to
money, race, &
writing.
Bungadoon!
   My kid watches Ninja turtles and they make about as
much sense as anything . . .

*   *   *

There had to be another way, to go about this, cracking down
the walls of the Bee. I haven't figured it out yet, but I'm trying, man, I'm trying. In the meantime, keep the faith, *gente*,
in whatever you're doing, keep doing it *your way*.
   This letter doesn't make much sense, but, nothing much
does.

Yours, Paz,
Walt
(Fuck-up in Fresno)

El Walt
Con
La Yoly
P/V

   Best piece of writing I've seen in Fresno. And there are famous poets in town!
   What vistas of the imagination it opens up!
   It's on the corner of Belmont and Fresno, unless it's been
erased by now, on an alley wall.
   El Walt con la Yoly P/V El Walt con la Yoly P/V El Walt con
la Yoly P/V. I hope he grows up to be a writer, who doesn't
appear in the Bee. I hope she gets out from under him, if she
wrote it, and asserts herself, on top. I hope they're both going
to school so they can both learn how to read and become glorious irresponsible citizens.

I hope I hope I hope . . . for things that are beyond the Bee's
ken.

Udderly,
Yours,
Ramírez

P.S. La Tuya.

RAÚL NIÑO

Moonless sky begins to change,
hues blending deep blue-grays
emerging lines of ocher,
fiery brow of an angry god
heaven and earth dividing.
These pallets of insomnia,
hesitant shades of summer's solstice.

The restless night of desire is over,
my lover sleeps in her foreign thoughts,
loosely tucked between thin sheets
the curve of her spine exposed to my memory,
the sovereignty of her bed drifting away.

Land-locked I watch as
navigating light fills her room,
familiar patterns returning,
textures gradually stretching,
cloths, furniture and floor,
waiting to be touched,
exposed, the blues
and grays.

My hands are restless dreamers
that awaken early,
seeking your geography

two hardy explorers
hiking over valleys and hills
of your warm terrain.
They need no light
these faithful adventurers
memory guides them
through receding shadows
of familiar textures,
that soft nostalgia
their only goal.

Sparrow songs measure this dim hour,
while a stubborn moon
still lolls in the sky,
a clipped thumbnail
remnant of a celestial manicure.
Gradually light returns,
naming all it touches,
giving shape to this cyclical dream.

Nothing is new, nothing is old,
each breath taken, has been taken,
texture of skin softens
as infants cry for their first meal,
wind sows seeds
as branches break and fall,
mountains turn to sand
as oceans greet their arrival.
There is nothing to lament,
what sages said
still echoes,
listen, sparrows know this.

My dawn
Is your dusk
Your eyes close
Mine open

Moon seduces oceans
To fill your shores
While the gravity of lovers
Strolls freely against all odds
Corralling history
Into the palms of fidelity
Soft laughter beneath your sky
Makes the long journey towards mine

My dusk
Is your dawn
My eyes close
Yours open

DIEGO VÁSQUEZ, JR.

NO, CLARENCE, NOT KAFKA, IT IS THE PRINCE

You must have
reread Machiavelli
recalling
Power
at
all
cost.

I will never believe
you
but it no longer
matters
cause you'll
be kicking ass
for
the rest
of my life.

I did enjoy
your
return
to brotherhood
for a
miraculous
few hours
where the twelve
white

men
asked
you
insensitive
questions
and of course
you
would not
answer
because you
had been
disrespected . . .

Right. Your Honor.
Men with your shade
of truth
cannot have
seasonal thoughts
for a beautiful woman
much less
about women
and of
their
rights
and privilege.
When Anita spoke,
your Christian
educated wife
sent you home
and before the vote,
Virginia wanted the kitchen
blinds shut tightly
so both of you could focus
and sing along

with almighty recordings
scored from battlefields
of good and evil.

Well, Clarence
you must've learned
from your private
sessions
that
to lie
for a position
on the Supreme
bench
is good . . .
and,
a woman
carrying
any truth
around her neck

GREETING A CARDINAL ON THE SONORAN DESERT

I was in between
a funeral
a busted romance
a new promise
of forever
and a red small
bird landed
two inches
from my burning face.
It hopped into the air

after a quick
conclusion
I was mad.

Bird—
I'm in love!
Come back
you can land
on my toes.
I will not move
nor breathe
until
you listen.

It returned
offering me
its brief
red
knowing
me as a sucker
for anything
that
beautiful

PALE GREEN EYES DID NOT CRY

Thomas Wolfe
meant
it
when he said
we could not
go home
again

nor find
the lost
key
opening the gates
on the lane
end
of silent
marching
men
knowing
they would
know
when
they
got
to the
place . . .

Thomas
paid
whores
junkies
girls
who would
never
read
his stuff
just
so
he could
look
in their eyes.

Most men
marry
and never
get
as close

ON THE VIOLATIONS OF POETRY

The first thing I read
to my baby
she was six days old
was an account
of Neruda
dragged
dying
from
his
Isla
Negra
home.

Don Pablo cried
and Matilde
said it was her
first time
ever—
to see
him
so.

Alma y sal
caressed his words
and we were tight
navigators
with him
as our
captain.

He left us Odas
sufficient
to displease
migrant powers
like builders
of Satellite
dishes south
of Santiago.

Neruda's last home
is surrounded
in the black coal
of a government installed
fence
and salt troughs of exiles
in a constant wave
returning to his house
bearing him gifts
of scrawled words
on the decaying fence.

CARLOS CUMPIÁN

LOCO CHUY RAPS WITH TONY ATOLE

Keep your theories out of my kitchen
if you don't want to hear me bitchin,
I know hot dogs have got red dye in 'em,
but that's my favorite carcinogen,
so go on munching with your
bird seed habit, living on a diet
made for rabbits, just keep your
tail out of my kitchen.
Flaco, I'm no animal lover,
so don't down rap my bloody steak,
and I might try your honey carrot cake,
I've worked hard all week that's why
I deserve this thick ice cream shake,
so what, I'll get fat,
big deal, a few pimples,
b.s., there's no relation
between eating meat and cancer.

Mira Tony, here's my answer,
a flip bird for thee, you,
you health store whore,
see if I care if too much protein
makes for dandruff,
or guzzling booze
might make me bald,

go on, keep your corn and beans
to your savage self,
I'll eat clean canned food
off the shelf.

Say ese, you carry brown nationalism
just a bit too far, promoting brown rice
over plain old white—
alright, I'll stop drinkin' rum and gin,
just as soon as the regular
moon tours begin,
but right now I'm on the pinche phone,
making an order for the pizza
to be mailed home,
I've had it with your macro-pedos,
you better be cool or
you'll be out like an eight-inch tie,
and if you don't use a microwave oven,
how you going to get everything hot,
using candles and a box of incense?
Tomorrow, breakfast is gonna be fried spam, eggs,
grape jam and toast, you better eat everything,
since I'm playing host.

OUR EVIL EMPIRE

*In the summer of 1965, African-Americans in Los Angeles
Watts district rioted for eleven days. A total of 35 deaths
were reported.*

There are times
when our city becomes
America's Beirut on the lake,
like that hot August weekend

when ambulances rushed
as if war had been launched
at the close of Friday's
six o'clock news.

Just who put out the call
so many would have to mourn
across the stretch of the city?
Because, more people were killed,
collected and carried off,
wrapped in stained body bags,
in less time than it took
to uproot the plotters
who staged a coup
against Gorbachev's
fading superpower rule.
While the dead are grieved,
washing away their
wasted blood
will go faster
than forgetting
all the life inside
sons and daughters,
sisters and brothers,
husbands and wives,
enemies and friends,
relatives and strangers,
that was stolen by
planned and spontaneous
acts of violence.

50 victims,
50 victims in one weekend,
some fell in stop-motion pose,

others squirmed and gasped
after the barrel-size blasts
went from Friday to Sunday.

Some people hid their kids
inside bathtubs to deflect
incoming strays,
some people lied to themselves
saying it was o.k.
to stay inside all day—
from the earliest rays
to the dark dream glow
of electrical starlight,
how many youngsters dashed past
unboarded windows
when weapons erupted and
lead sprayed across
the width of crowded projects,
parks and streets,
making it a life-or-death choice
for parents to go get
milk at the store,
as the reverberating voice
that filled the air
forced dozens to hunker
down alongside the absent sun
as more cracks of guns found another
to be laid out cold
naked toe-tagged at the morgue.

Aren't you sick
of aftermath reports—
where the guy with the tie
stands outside the

coroner's door,
loosens his collar,
and all he can say is,
"Motives are being sought . . ."

But you know what,
there'd be national guardsmen
hunting down the killers
if even a quarter of
those being shot
lived in lily-white
Winnetka.

Venus Envy

Yes, women have more freedom than men, when it comes to clothing, thought Dinú as Víctor admired her dress made of lace, velvet, silk and linen. "Gorgeous dress," he commented. "It's unfair that men cannot wear such things. Look at me, white shirt, gray pants, perhaps an interesting colorful tie at the most; it's not fair; women can wear beautiful things like your dress; what is it made of? Where is it from?" Víctor touched her dress with curiosity and envy. "It's from Paris," she answered, a bit self-consciously. The dress was an ocean green with a V-neckline and V-backline cut very low but lined with lace, allowing her skin to show through. Dinú resented Víctor for making such remarks because she felt it was similar to the sort of envy that sometimes goes on among women, the kind of competitiveness that she detested. Besides, she imagined that he envied the female gender, that he would want to be a woman, a feminine one for sure, and she liked masculine men, content with their virility, who, without being macho or degrading feminine matters, viewed such lace and jewelry not as a requirement but an option for women.

Dinú had already noticed a few "feminine" gestures in Víctor, as when he moved his hands as he talked or the way he described his *yegua*: "that horse of mine, she's got a biiiiiiiig aaass," with his mouth hanging open and tilting his head from side to side. They had barely kissed, but Dinú knew that she was not attracted to him, despite the fact that he was a good-looking, progressive Mexican who had struggled during his medical career because of financial difficulties. Dinú had been more fortunate having had nouveau riche parents who helped out in many ways. Despite some background differences, Dinú and Víctor shared many things in common, but she was not interested in pursuing the relationship. He would feel rejected and she would perhaps regret that they ever went out in the first place.

Dinú had a part-time Jewish lover with whom she discussed everything without censorship. "Isaac, do you ever envy women because they can wear pretty dresses, jewelry, make-up and all of that?" After a short pause, Isaac replied: "I've told you before, I'd like to be able to be a woman for a day, wear a mini-skirt to a bar and get fucked by a man. Like I've said before, women have it better sexually." "Why?" she asked. "Is it because you believe the penis is superior and therefore women are privileged because they can enjoy it inside of them?" Dinú waited skeptically for Isaac's answer. "No, I just think it's easier for women; they don't have to worry about having to get an erection or keeping it; they can fake it, men can't. Women have fewer sexual problems than men; women can just go to a bar and someone will approach them, whereas men don't get approached by women. Women have it much easier finding sex; men have to resort to paying when they can't get it. If a woman wants sex, she can get it pretty easily, especially if the man's had a few beers or if he's desperate." Dinú interrupts: "But, women are not satisfied by just any man they're going to meet at a bar; men can block off a lot of garbage and get inside someone's mouth or inside anything and come and they're satisfied; female orgasm is more complex. I think that it's a stereotype to say that 'women fake it'. As far as I am concerned, I would only fake *not* having one so that the guy would do me again." He responds: "Nevertheless, men have to worry about performing or they have premature ejaculation or some can't come at all." Dinú adds: "So, you've wanted to wear dresses before? That's disgusting." Isaac: "Sure, a lot of men want to dress up and want to feel what it's like to be a woman, but my days of wearing skirts, oh, they're over, that was a long time ago." He ended the sentence with a chuckle to allow for a bit of disbelief.

After hanging up, Dinú remembered how her first lover, a young and vain Venezuelan, had a small tin box filled with crayon-like make-up of eight different colors. She asked Willie why he had such make-up in his bathroom and he explained that he liked to paint his face every now and then. She then had selected the purple "crayon" and dabbed some on her eyelids.

Dinú dialed Isaac's number once again. "Isaac, you must be crazy. I was thinking about our conversation and I am convinced sex is much easier for men. For example, of all the lovers I had before I met my ex-husband, I did not have an orgasm with any of them and they all had one. Why? Because, as you know, only 30 percent of women can have an orgasm while having intercourse alone, unless, that is, her clitoris is manually stimulated during coitus. When I was younger I didn't know better and they didn't either or didn't bother. Only one, I believe, ever initiated giving me oral sex and I almost came, I remember, but he stopped just right before I climaxed; I guess he got tired. If I go to a bar right now and pick up a man, what percentage is there that he'll know how to please a woman? Whereas if you go pick up a woman, well, it's true, you may not be able to get it up but . . . well, I won't speak for the man, but like I said, all the men I was with reached orgasm, so I prove my point that female orgasm takes more skill. When I met my ex-husband I thought that he was the only man in the world with whom I could have an orgasm. Little did I know, but that's to prove to you what a bunch of nincompoops I had had and they're still out there, especially the real young ones who have a lot to learn. As they get older and their dick's not as hard, they learn to compensate, I guess. I know that you, Isaac, get off on making women feel good, but you are exceptional and that's why you're still my part-time lover after two-and-a-half years." She took a sip of Chamomile tea which sat on a book beside her bed. Isaac replied: "Even if you thought I was weird at first?" "Yes, and you're still unusual but that's why you make me laugh. You know, Isaac-o, for those people you know who believe in God, you can tell them that God sure was macho when he made orgasm easier for the man. He knew that was the way to control women, because this way, they would not openly seek out sex because (1) they'd get pregnant and (2) their chances of having an orgasm with a caveman were only 30 percent, under the best conditions. Why didn't he place the clitoris just a wee bit higher or make it more protruding so that women would have orgasm 100 percent of the time through intercourse?" "But, Dinúbelle, with me you have up to four orgasms in one night, so what's your complaint?" "Yes, Isaac-y, but you think cavemen believed in foreplay? They probably just hopped on their 'lady' after a hard day's work." Isaac chuckled: "Well, of course, we all know that most cultures in the world don't take into account female sexuality; some of them even force women to get circumcised, preventing female orgasm." "As I was telling you, 'Sac, God was born with a penis so he figured he could abuse his privilege and thus created the Virgin Mary concept." Isaac always had something to say about Dinú's Mexican ancestry: "Except for your people, who have that Guadalupee Indian Virgin." Dinú: "Right, but don't you get it? God had a castrated-complex and wanted to get back at women. He was a misogynist." Isaac: "You called me a misogynist when you met me." "Yes, Isaac, and now you're my god, ha, ha!" "All right, Dinúbelle. You can re-create your own creation myth and tell me about it later. I'll talk to you tomorrow."

Dinú looked at the green dress hanging in her closet: French lace with satin, silk and linen, flowing skirt and low neckline, and the "freedom" to wear it. The cotton balls smeared with black mascara and eye-liner, which she had rubbed off her eyes, lay dormant in the trash can. She crawled into the light-blue flannel sheets, ruminating on how her own creation myth would be.

About the Contributors

PATRICIA BLANCO
was born in Phoenix and has worked as a dancer, stagehand, and bilingual teacher. Her work has appeared in *Mirrors Beneath the Earth: Short Fiction by Chicano Writers*.

DAN COOPER ALARCÓN
is from Menasha, Wisconsin. He worked as a newspaper reporter before studying creative writing with Patricia Hample, Sandra Benítez, and Grace Paley at the University of Minnesota, and his fiction has appeared in the *Wisconsin Academy Review* and *City Pages*. He is currently an assistant professor of English at the University of Arizona.

CARLOS CUMPIÁN
is a coordinator of Movimiento Artístico Chicano's literary efforts in Chicago. His first book of poetry, *Coyote Sun* (MARCH/ Abrazo Press, 1990), is now in its second printing. Cumpián has been published in numerous journals and anthologies including *Fiesta en Aztlán*, *Third World*, *Emergency Tacos*, and recently *After Aztlán*. He has also published in the journals, *Exquisite Corpse*, *Spoon River Quarterly*, and *Literati Internazionale*.

ROBERTA FERNÁNDEZ
was born and reared in Laredo, Texas. She received a Ph.D. in Romance Languages and Literatures from the University of California, Berkeley. She is currently an assistant professor in Hispanic Studies at the University of Houston, where she is also an editor at Arte Público Press. Her work has appeared in numerous publications including *The Massachusetts Review*,

Fem (Mexico City), and *The Americas Review*. Multicultural Publishers Exchange selected her book, *Intaglio: A Novel in Six Stories*, as the best book of fiction for 1991. She has been named to the Texas Institute of Letters.

ODILIA GALVÁN RODRÍGUEZ,

originally from the south side of Chicago, has been a political activist and writer since age fifteen. She worked as an organizer for the United Farm Workers' Union and supported the American Indian and other civil rights movements. She currently lives with her son, Hawk, in Berkeley, California. Her work has been published in several magazines and anthologies.

STEPHEN D. GUTIÉRREZ

has published in a variety of magazines, including *The Americas Review, Puerto del Sol, Saguaro,* and *The Santa Monica Review*. An essay, *"bombing out . . . memories from an M.F.A. program,"* is forthcoming in *Notebook/Cuaderno*. He teaches creative writing at California State University, Hayward.

ROLANDO HINOJOSA

is a prolific writer who has authored ten prose fiction works and a long narrative poem which together comprise his Klail City Death Trip Series. He won the Quinto Sol Prize for Literature in 1973 for *Estampas del valle y otras obras*, and in 1976 he was awarded a prestigious Premio Casa de las Américas (Cuba) for *Klail City y sus alrededores*. He is a Professor at the University of Texas, where he holds an endowed chair in the Department of English.

JOEL HUERTA

was born and raised in Edinburg, Texas, in the Lower Rio Grande Valley. He is a graduate of Rice University and the Creative Writing Program at the University of Arizona. He is currently a doctoral student at the University of Texas in Austin.

RITA MAGDALENO

was born in Augsburg, Germany. Her work has appeared
in *New Frontiers: A Journal for Women, Puerto del Sol,* and
the *Taos Review* as well as in several anthologies, including
Named in Stone and Sky: An Arizona Anthology. She has been
a featured reader at the Bisbee Poetry Festival and the Inter-
American Book Fair in San Antonio. She is a 1992–94 Roster
Artist for the Arizona Commission on the Arts.

PAT MORA'S

three books of poetry, *Chants, Borders,* and *Communion,* are
published by Arte Público Press. Her book of personal essays,
Nepantla: Essays from the Land in the Middle, will be published by the University of New Mexico Press in 1993. Her
children's books are forthcoming from Macmillan, Knopf,
and Clarion Books.

RAÚL NIÑO

is the author of *Breathing Light,* published by MARCH/Abrazo
Press in 1991. His poetry has appeared in the anthologies
Emergency Tacos (MARCH/Abrazo Press, 1989) and *New Chi-
cana/Chicano Writing I* (University of Arizona Press, 1992),
and in the literary journals *TONANTZIN, Hammers,* and *The
Guadalupe Review.*

ANA PERCHES

was born in Chihuahua and raised in Juárez/El Paso. She received her Ph.D from the University of New Mexico and is
now assistant professor of Spanish at the University of Arizona. She teaches Spanish American and Chicano literatures
and Spanish for native speakers. Her current research deals
with Chicano ethnicity in literary texts.

MARY HELEN PONCE

a native of Califas, writes of the Chicana experience. Her
works include *Taking Control* and *The Wedding,* a fifties

novel. Her book *Hoyt Street: Autobiography* will be published by the University of New Mexico Press in 1993. A monograph, "Five Hispanic New Mexican Women Writers, 1878–1991: Short Biography," is forthcoming from the Center for Regional Studies at the University of New Mexico.

ORLANDO RAMÍREZ

is a native of Tucson. He was graduated from Yale University, then moved to San José, California, where he spent several years working with Mango Publications. In 1979 he won first prize for poetry in the University of California, Irvine Chicano Literary Contest. Presently he lives in San Diego.

DIEGO VÁSQUEZ

lives in St. Paul, Minnesota, where he has been selected to read his poetry for various public readings, radio programs, and video productions. In 1990, he participated in the Loft's Hispanic Inroads series.